WHAT DO EMPLOYERS WANT?

WHAT DO EMPLOYERS WANT?

A Guide for Library Science Students

Priscilla K. Shontz and Richard A. Murray

Foreword by G. Kim Dority
Illustrations by Robert N. Klob

 LIBRARIES UNLIMITED

AN IMPRINT OF ABC-CLIO, LLC
Santa Barbara, California • Denver, Colorado • Oxford, England

Library of Congress Cataloging-in-Publication Data

Shontz, Priscilla K., 1965–
    What do employers want? : a guide for library science students / Priscilla K. Shontz and Richard A. Murray ; foreword by G. Kim Dority ; illustrations by Robert N. Klob.
        pages cm
    Includes bibliographical references and index.
    ISBN 978–1–59884–828–1 (pbk.) — ISBN 978–1–59884–829–8 (ebook)
1. Library science—Vocational guidance—United States. 2. Librarians—Employment—United States. I. Murray, Richard A. (Richard Allen), 1973– II. Title.
Z682.35.V62S48   2012
020.23′73—dc23   2012005693

ISBN: 978–1–59884–828–1
EISBN: 978–1–59884–829–8

16 15 14 13 12   1 2 3 4 5

This book is also available on the World Wide Web as an eBook.
Visit www.abc-clio.com for details.

Libraries Unlimited
An Imprint of ABC-CLIO, LLC

ABC-CLIO, LLC
130 Cremona Drive, P.O. Box 1911
Santa Barbara, California 93116-1911

This book is printed on acid-free paper (∞)

Manufactured in the United States of America

For Laura and Sophie, who inspire me to stretch
in unanticipated directions.
P. K. S.

For Debbie, the best sister I could ever ask for.
R. A. M.

CONTENTS

FOREWORD

Every year, more than 5,000 students graduate from North America's 63 ALA-accredited master's programs in library and/or information science (LIS). They may go into fields as diverse as taxonomy development, school librarianship, special-collection archives, information architecture, adult services for public libraries, competitive intelligence, community information services, online content development, or literally hundreds of other career directions.

What they all have in common, however, is that they are going to be seeking jobs in what may be one of the most daunting, competitive employment landscapes any of us have ever seen (including those of us who have lived through a couple of recessions). Needless to say, *any* competitive edge you can lay your hands on to more effectively position yourself with potential employers is a good thing.

What Do Employers Want? is a *very* good thing.

Based on interviews with a wide range of employers who've hired (or not) many LIS graduates over the years, the practical, proven advice authors Priscilla Shontz and Richard Murray provide in this book will help you start building your job prospects in graduate school and then give you a fighting chance to not only identify where the good jobs are, but also to successfully land one of them.

Correctly assuming that most LIS graduate programs are strong on teaching information skills but a bit weak on what it takes to get hired in a difficult job market, Priscilla and Rich lay out the "while-you're-a-student" basics. What should you be doing in grad school to start creating job opportunities? What are the key elements of networking you need to understand

and master? What about building a professional brand while you're still a student? What other skills can you develop in grad school that will help you differentiate yourself from the hundreds of other job applicants you may be going up against once you've gotten that diploma?

The result of this wise counsel: every tuition dollar you've spent (or are currently spending) is much likelier to lead directly to a career payoff.

The second half of *What Do Employers Want?* is equally valuable and equally important. In teaching a graduate course in alternative LIS career paths for ten years at the University of Denver, I've found that while my students are almost always excellent at being students, the effort they put in to achieve this lofty goal distracts them from a critical insight: the purpose of being an MLIS student for a year or two is to then get a job (or, more likely, a series of them) and support themselves as information professionals.

Priscilla and Rich effectively address this issue in the book's second half. Calling on their personal experience as LIS professionals as well as insights shared by those interviewed employers, the authors' advice is practical and knowledgeable. The fact that it reflects the preferences of your potential hiring managers makes it just that much more valuable.

Pretty much everyone now realizes that while an MLIS can guarantee you many, many career options, it in no way guarantees you job opportunities. You have to create those for yourself. This book will help you understand what steps you need to take to start creating those opportunities and then how to successfully turn job opportunities into job offers.

Kim Dority
President, Dority & Associates, Inc.
Author, *Rethinking Information Work*

PREFACE

Library and information science students often complain that their graduate programs do not give them the information they need to find their first professional position. In a tight job market, more and more recent graduates struggle to find the jobs they hoped for, sometimes leading them to question their decisions to enter the profession. In our roles as authors, editors, librarians, and invited speakers, we frequently hear the same job search questions from students and recent graduates:

How can I improve my resume, application, cover letter, or interview skills?

What can I do to set myself apart from the competition?

What do employers want?

In this book, we offer career advice gathered from employers and experienced professionals involved in the hiring process. What goes on behind the scenes during a job search? What turns employers off when they evaluate an application? What attributes do they value in an employee?

Learn what you can do while you're in graduate school to maximize your chances of getting a professional position when you graduate. Although this book is geared toward students, the advice may also help prospective students, new graduates, career changers, and others looking for work in the library and information field.

The book is divided into two major sections: the student experience and the job search process. The first section includes strategies for increasing your value as a potential employee while you are still a student. The second section offers practical guidance for navigating your search for an entry-level professional position. Throughout the book, we have quoted many librarians and information professionals; their affiliations are listed only the first time they are mentioned.

We'd love to hear from you. Please visit LIScareer.com for more practical career advice from information professionals, and as you progress in your career, we hope you'll consider writing an article for the site to share your experiences with others.

ACKNOWLEDGMENTS

We'd like to thank Kim Dority for her constant encouragement; she has been a wonderful mentor to both of us throughout this process. We're thrilled that she wrote the foreword for this book.

We're grateful to the many people who helped us create this book. Our acquisitions editor, Blanche Woolls, patiently answered our many questions and provided helpful advice as we worked. Wendy Israel and Holly Riggs read and commented on early drafts. Tiffany Eatman Allen and Susanne Markgren contributed special essays. Priscilla's dad, Robert Klob, drew the illustrations. Anne Brûlé and Ellen Symons indexed the book. Emma Bailey, Elizabeth Claeys, and Arathi Pillai helped make the book a reality.

We'd especially like to thank the numerous colleagues out there who shared their career advice. You'll see many of their names throughout this book, and there are countless others who provided invaluable insights.

Priscilla would like to thank her husband, David, for his love and support; her parents for their constant encouragement; and her children, Laura and Sophie, for their joyfulness and curiosity. She also appreciates Sai Boeker, Keri Richards, Pen Anderson, Brian Laird, and Cheryl Brisbane for listening, understanding, and making her laugh.

Rich would like to thank his parents for always being there; his current and former colleagues, particularly Beth Doyle and Noah Huffman, for making work more fun; Rosalyn Raeford for being such a supportive and inspiring boss; and Mark Rifkin for making everything happier and brighter.

CHAPTER 1

What Employers Want

Lemon, we're not just hiring an actor, we're hiring a coworker, a human being, and I say we hire the one who lives by the code of the robot: Care, Love, Live.

30 Rock, 2009

So, you're in library school. You love your classes and are really excited about becoming a librarian. You know this is the perfect field for you. Maybe you've chosen to enter the information science field as a second career. You study hard, earn a 4.0 GPA, walk across the stage at commencement, and receive your MLS degree.

And then what?
You send out a few resumes. And a few more. And maybe a *lot* more.
And you wait.
And wait.
Hey, what's up with that? Why isn't anyone calling you for an interview?
How can you be expected to compete with applicants who have more experience than you?
Was earning your graduate degree worth all that money and time?
Sure, you learned all about Ranganathan and reference queries and Library 2.0 in school, but did anyone teach you how to find a real job in the real world?

Unfortunately, we hear depressing stories like this all the time. Especially in a tight job market, recent graduates may struggle to find jobs, which may lead them to question their decisions to enter the field of library and information science.

Wouldn't you like to know what employers are really looking for? How can you make yourself more attractive to a prospective employer? How can you stand out in a job search?

You can take many steps while you're still a student that will prepare you to succeed in your job search and career. We've collected career advice and insights into the hiring process from employers and experienced professionals. They (and we) have been where you are; we hope the ideas in this book may help you make a successful transition from student to happily employed information professional.

YOU CAN'T START TOO EARLY ...

It may sound ridiculous, but you should start thinking about your first professional position as soon as you start taking classes. No, we don't advise you to send out resumes in your first semester, but thinking ahead about your career while you are a student can help you prepare to be successful in your job search when you graduate. If you work hard, plan thoughtfully—and maybe have a little luck—you might even line up a job before you receive your diploma!

That's not to say you'll breeze through your first (or any) job search. Job hunts are enormously stressful tasks that take a huge amount of time and effort. They're also often mysterious and frustrating experiences for applicants who wait for what seems like eternity to hear (or not) from prospective employers. In chapter 6, employers demystify the process a little by sharing what happens on their side of the hiring process.

... BUT IT'S NOT TOO LATE

If you've graduated recently—or not so recently—and still don't have a job, all is not lost. The principles behind finding and getting an entry-level position don't change drastically after the ink on your diploma dries. If you've been searching for a while and still haven't found that first job, you should reevaluate the tactics you've been using. It may be that you've fallen into one or more of the common pitfalls that trip up many job seekers. Perhaps rethinking your resume, cover letter, and interviewing techniques may help. Be proactive about gaining experience, skills, and contacts that may make you more appealing in the eyes of potential employers.

WHAT DO EMPLOYERS LOOK FOR?

A job search is a lot like dating: you're both looking for the right match. When you're searching for an entry-level job, you're a lot less picky than the employer: sometimes you might even feel like pleading, "I'll take *any* job!" At this stage, you do have to be flexible with your wants and needs, but you should also look for a job and work environment that mesh well with your career goals, work interests, and personality.

Employers often have the opposite problem: they may receive hundreds of applications for a single entry-level position. In this situation, what will they do to narrow down the huge pile of resumes they have to sift through? What attributes are employers looking for? What qualities do they value in a candidate or a new employee? They recognize that you're going to become part of their work family. Employers typically want to hire someone who will mesh well with the other people in their organization, add positive energy, and offer fresh ideas in a tactful manner.

We asked numerous employers, "What are some key skills or attributes that you typically look for in a potential employee?" Most talked more about personality traits and soft skills such as enthusiasm, initiative, innovation, communication, flexibility, and collaboration than they did about academic knowledge. So, as a potential job candidate, how can you develop those highly desired qualities and demonstrate them to an employer in a cover letter, resume, and interview?

LOVE WHAT YOU DO

"Eagerness makes new grads stand out, so show that enthusiasm," said Dawn Krause (Texas State Library). This doesn't mean jumping up and down on the interview table. Use your cover letter, resume, and interview to express how excited you are about becoming part of the library community and, in particular, how interested you are in doing that particular job at that particular institution.

Applying for jobs you're genuinely excited about will certainly increase your chances of getting an offer. If you're applying for a job as an instruction librarian and you don't like speaking to groups, that will be apparent in the interview, and you probably won't get the job. (Even if you do, you'll probably be miserable.) Don't get carried away and scare off your interviewers with your "rah rah" vibe. You don't want them to feel like they need to go lie down in a dark room after they've talked to you, but if you're truly excited about the job, your interviewers will feel your positive energy.

Don't be afraid to show that you love what you do. "See the profession as a lively, growing, interesting place to be," encouraged Diane Calvin (Ball State University).

ACCENTUATE THE POSITIVE

Nurture a positive attitude and let employers see it. "I look for someone with a positive personality and a service orientation," said Nancy Agafetei (Harris County Public Library System).

Nobody wants to hire Debbie Downer. Employers are looking for someone who will be pleasant to work with and someone who will respond to adverse situations with a positive, proactive spirit—not someone who will give up, sit back, and wait for others to handle a problem or who will complain about every situation.

Kim Dority (Dority & Associates, Inc.) said, "Employers look for qualities such as self-management, intelligence, positive attitude, ability and willingness to learn quickly, ability to work well with colleagues, engagement, and energy."

A job search can often be discouraging; don't focus on the rejections. Keep your eye on the goal, stay optimistic, and keep moving forward. After all, everyone can't say yes all the time. Use the obstacles and disappointments to reshape your job search strategy if necessary. Instead of focusing on what didn't happen, focus on what you can do to make it work the next time.

TAKE THE INITIATIVE

Employers look for employees who show that they are willing to try new things and do anything that's needed. "When I evaluate a candidate, I'm looking for a demonstrated interest in continuing to learn new skills, a demonstrated interest in trying new things, a willingness to experiment (to succeed and fail), and an overall enthusiasm for being in a learning environment," said Beth Doyle (Duke University).

Librarians must constantly adapt to changing technologies. In most workplaces, you'll be expected to hit the ground (almost) running. Your potential coworkers want to feel that you'll be able to learn new things quickly. Sometimes you'll be expected to learn new technologies or resources in order to teach your fellow librarians. What's more, you need to learn things without being prompted. Be "quick to learn, self-motivated, assertive, and collegial," said Chris Nolan (Trinity University).

How can you demonstrate initiative and innovation to a prospective employer? If you don't have a lot of library experience, look at what you've done in previous careers or extracurricular activities. What have you done in addition to earning your MLS degree? Showing these additional activities, experiences, or skills on your resume can demonstrate that you've gone beyond the minimal requirement of going to library school. "I look for initiative in volunteer work; travel; trying new things; teaching, whether it be coaching, training other employees in a retail situation, teaching English overseas," Nancy George (Salem State University) said. "I also like to see some sort of experience working in a library (internship, public library, volunteer work in high school, or anything)."

Be willing to do whatever is needed, even if it's not a glamorous task. No one wants to hear you say, "That's not my job." Pitch in when you see a need. "We do not necessarily hire professionals with the most experience," said Rosa Liu (National Institute of Standards and Technology). "We hire those with a willingness to learn, openness to explore solutions, ability to work as a team member, and ability to be a self-starter."

PLAY WELL WITH OTHERS

Do you remember being evaluated on your kindergarten school report card for "playing well with others"? Well, this skill is just as important (and sometimes as challenging) in your career as it was when you were a child. Employers repeatedly mentioned that they look for a team player: someone who collaborates, adapts, and communicates well with others.

In any job you'll work with a lot of different personalities, including your coworkers, supervisors, and the clients or patrons that you serve. Even if you don't work in a public services-oriented position, you will interact with people every day. Lorene Flanders (University of West Georgia) said, "I look for enthusiasm for serving students and faculty and a depth of understanding how the library supports the campus and community. Whether people work in public service or behind the scenes, they need to be approachable and enthusiastic, and they must enjoy working with others."

Employers want to hire people who will cooperate with and contribute to the team they are joining. "Many of our projects are team-based and it is critical to the success of the project that the candidate contributes his or her part," said Rosa Liu. Connie Foster (Western Kentucky University) emphasized the "ability to work within a team environment, excellent communication skills, and the ability to manage promotion and tenure requirements."

As a team member, you'll have to get things done, sometimes working with challenging coworkers or doing projects or tasks in a way that you wouldn't have chosen to do them. "I look for evidence of a cooperative attitude, flexibility and adaptability, and an ability to think creatively," said Clint Chamberlain (University of Texas at Arlington). Susan Davis (University at Buffalo, SUNY) added, "I look for an engaging personality (will work well with others), good attention to detail, and the ability to learn and master new skills."

Employees who communicate in a professional, clear, positive, diplomatic, and tactful manner are highly valued. John Lehner (University of Houston) noted that he looks for "excellent oral and written communication skills, the ability to work collaboratively, and enthusiasm and interest in the position." Jenifer Abramson (UCLA) also listed "flexibility, creativity, and excellent verbal and written communication skills" as highly desired attributes.

FACE THE FUTURE

Employers also look for candidates who are comfortable with emerging technologies and trends. "When interviewing, I look for technical skills, written and oral communication skills, and flexibility," said Teri Switzer

(University of Colorado at Colorado Springs). As a new graduate you are often more aware of what's new in the field. In fact, your new employer will probably expect you to bring technical savvy simply because you just finished school. Use your time in library school to hone your technical skills, develop good learning habits that will help you keep up with new technology, and sharpen your perspective on the future of the field.

On your resume, list your technical proficiencies and include links to online examples of your work. "Tech skills definitely stand out," agreed Dawn Krause.

> If you can, put together a portfolio of the projects you've done in library school and put it online. I'm talking about presentations, screencasts, blogs, Web pages or pathfinders you've created, even videos. New grads tend to be very adept in these areas and libraries need these multimedia and social media skills. Also, this shows that you've taken initiative and put together a body of work that speaks about who you are as a person. Just make sure it's all appropriate content for the library world and is not too opinionated so you don't alienate anyone.

In addition to demonstrating technical skills, show that you're familiar with trends in information science. Jill Emery (Portland State University) said she looks for candidates who show "a knowledge of current standards in use, the ability to articulate current library trends beyond the buzzwords, and demonstrated research skills shown by research about the organization and employees with whom the candidate is interviewing."

Read as much as you can in library and information science literature, publications from other disciplines, and non-academic news sources to become well-versed on trends and practices in the information field. Talk with practicing librarians and those employed in alternative careers to learn more about what real-life information professionals do. Attend information science meetings and conferences if you're able. Learn as much about your profession as you can.

"The most important thing is to make your learning part of your life," said Judine Slaughter (United Black Writers Association). "Show you are not just getting a degree, but you are truly interested in the library field."

MAXIMIZE YOUR "HIRABILITY"

Don't wait until your last semester in school to start thinking about your career. Getting your MLS degree does not guarantee you a job; it's simply the minimum requirement for most positions. You'll often compete with hundreds of other applicants for the same jobs, so you need to improve your odds. Do *more* while you're in school so that you'll stand out from the crowd of other new graduates and experienced professionals.

"The most important thing you can do now for your career is to see everything as being unified," urged Ava Iuliano (Florida International University). "Resist the urge to compartmentalize things into 'what I have to do for grad school' and 'what I have to do to find a job.' The faster you unify both of these concepts, the easier your transition into the job market will be."

Make the most of your time as a student to gain knowledge, skills, and vision from practical experience as well as from your coursework. Many new graduates have little real experience working in a library or other relevant organization. Every bit of experience you have will help you rise above the masses applying for your target job. In fact, your job history will almost certainly have more to do with your employment prospects than your graduate or undergraduate grades.

Pursue professional opportunities and extracurricular activities. When evaluating a pool of applicants who have similar work experience and educational achievements, employers look at the "extras" such as presentations, publications, professional involvement, technical skills, and language proficiencies. Expand your evolving network of friends, teachers, and colleagues to help you navigate your job search and your new profession.

Learn to market your knowledge and skills effectively through resumes, cover letters, and interviews. Emphasize your energy and vision. Make the most of your transferable skills.

Above all, stay positive and be proactive. Looking for a job is sometimes discouraging, but don't throw up your hands and give up. Actively managing your professional life now, as a student or recent graduate, will help you increase your chances of launching your career more quickly.

SECTION 1

The Student Experience

CHAPTER 2

Your MLS Education

Bart, don't make fun of grad students. They just made a terrible life choice.

The Simpsons, 2005

Earning a master's in library or information science is not just about racking up the required number of credit hours and maybe writing a thesis or passing comprehensive exams. You should design your school experience thoughtfully, with an eye towards the career you want to have after you finish. Managing your education mindfully can help you better prepare for your future job searches and career. This book is not about how to decide whether you want to go to library school, or how to pick a program once you've made that decision. However, many students who are already in school find themselves wondering whether they've chosen the right one, or whether there are things they need to do while they're in school based on the choice they've made. Sometimes recent graduates, especially if they're facing a long job search, wonder if the school they attended is putting them at a disadvantage. We'll touch briefly on some of these questions before moving on to things you can do while you're in school to make the most of your education and improve your odds of getting a job when you graduate.

DOES IT MATTER WHETHER I GO TO A TOP-RATED SCHOOL?

Students and recent graduates often wonder how important it is to attend a "top tier" (whatever that means) library school. The programs ranked highly by *U.S. News and World Report* and other sources usually trumpet that accolade loudly. So does it really matter which school you go to?

If all other things are equal, then going to a top-ranked school is probably better. That said, all other things are practically never equal. The idea of Job Applicant A and Job Applicant B, who are identical in every way except that A went to a higher-ranked school than B, is pretty much a fairy tale. There are always numerous differences between candidates, even freshly minted MLS graduates: work experience, professional involvement, special skills, personality, even the quality of their resumes and cover letters. That's a big part of what this book is about: how to tip the scale in your favor.

Yes, on a superficial level, going to Famous State University is probably preferable to going to University That Nobody Has Ever Heard Of. "The library school isn't a big deciding factor, but experienced search committee members form opinions about library schools after a while," Diane Calvin said. But from most employers' perspectives, where you went to school is not nearly as important as what you did while you were there.

So if choosing a program that's top ranked isn't so important, then what is? If you're applying for library jobs in the United States, the most important thing is that you attend a library school that's accredited by the American Library Association (ALA). When you look at job vacancy announcements—which you should be doing constantly while you're in school—you will very frequently see the phrase "ALA-accredited MLS" or some variant thereof in the "Required Qualifications" section. ALA's Office for Accreditation regularly reviews MLS programs across the United States and Canada to make sure they meet a number of basic standards, including curriculum and course offerings, qualifications of faculty, facilities, and funding levels. Not all MLS programs pass, and if this happens, a school is allowed to continue accepting and graduating students, but those students' degrees are considered unaccredited by ALA. If your degree is not from an ALA-accredited program, many libraries will not (or cannot) consider you for professional employment. In some states, you're required to have an ALA-accredited degree to be allowed to work as a public or school librarian. Making sure your degree is from an ALA-accredited institution will give you the most flexibility when seeking employment; this should be considered the baseline when you choose a program.

You should consider a number of other factors when you're choosing a library school:

- What opportunities will there be to get work experience while you're in school? Does the program have a placement office or other similar service to help students find jobs?
- How much will it cost, and what financial aid is available? Most librarians don't make a ton of money, especially early in their careers, so ask yourself whether going into a lot of debt while you're

in school makes sense and is something you would be comfortable with. The most expensive schools are not necessarily the best!

- How many credit hours does the program require, and how many semesters do most students take to complete it?
- What specializations (if any) does the program offer, and how do those match your interests?
- What courses are required and what electives are offered?
- Does the program cater to students who want to work full time while they're earning their degrees? (This may or may not be a factor for you based on your situation and plans.) Some library schools specifically target nontraditional or returning students by offering many courses during the evening or on weekends, while other schools cater mostly to full-time students and offer most or all of their courses during more traditional hours.
- Does the program require writing a master's paper or thesis, and/or taking a comprehensive exam at the end of the program? The presence or absence of these things doesn't automatically make a program better or worse—it's just something to keep in mind as you're comparing schools.
- How many of the faculty members are tenured and in what subjects do they specialize? Who are the adjunct instructors who teach there, where do they work, and in which areas are they practitioners? Adjunct faculty—usually those who have full-time jobs working in a library, archive, or other information environment—can be some of the best teachers, because they can often give you realistic advice about what it's like as a working professional and how to get a job when you finish. They may also know more people who are currently working in local libraries, which may make them more likely to be able to help you find internships or other work opportunities while you're in school. Ideally, you should have a combination of full-time faculty and adjunct instructors in your MLS program.

DOES IT MATTER WHETHER I GO TO SCHOOL ONLINE OR IN PERSON?

Students who are earning their MLS degrees partially or completely online often wonder whether employers will look negatively upon their degrees when they enter the job market. When online degree programs were introduced, many librarians were wary of them; they often questioned whether students coming out of online programs were as well-prepared as students coming from traditional environments. Today, however, online education, not just in library and information science but in many disciplines, has become a major part of higher education in North America. Professionals working in many environments and fields earned their degrees online. Frequently librarians don't know whether their colleagues earned their degrees online or in person. In fact, because most academic libraries have had to adjust their collections and services to accommodate the fact that their students may be earning part or all of their degrees online, librarians who have personal experience as distance learners can provide valuable input.

All that said, however, if you earn your degree online, you will have to work harder at certain things than students in traditional programs. For example, getting relevant work experience while you're attending an online library school can be challenging. As we'll discuss in the next chapter, getting practical experience while you're in school is absolutely critical to your future success as a librarian. Many library schools have placement offices with staff members who are familiar with local libraries and librarians; it's often easier for them to help local students find jobs than to help faraway students find jobs where they live. Find out whether your school offers placement services for distance education students. If you live in a very small town or remote location, earning your degree virtually from your living room is fabulous, but can you find an internship in your area? If you aren't able to move to go to school, will you be mobile when you finish your degree and begin job hunting? Think creatively: are there "virtual internships" you can do?

Also remember that librarianship is a people profession. As librarians, we connect people with information. Even if you're not on the front line helping patrons at a reference desk or other service point, you will be working and making connections with other people. Ask yourself how you will be able to get that kind of interaction if you're going to class online. It's by no means impossible, but as a distance learner, you may have to work harder to make these kinds of connections and experiences happen.

WHICH CLASSES SHOULD I TAKE?

So now you're in school and you may be wondering what classes you should take. The course catalog can seem overwhelming with its abundance of choices, many of which will probably sound interesting; if they don't, you should be asking yourself if you've made the right career choice. A few of them probably won't interest you, and you probably won't even understand what some of them are about. Don't let this worry you; as you progress through the program, you'll learn more about different aspects of librarianship and how they connect.

Certain core classes will probably be required, so you won't have a choice about whether or not to take them. These typically include courses like reference, collection development, cataloging, and management, although they may be called other names like "Provision of User Services" or "Organization of Information." These have been the fundamental areas and concepts of librarianship forever, and they still are, so even if your program doesn't require you to take them, *take them anyway*. You may never work on a reference desk or catalog a book a day in your life, but you will constantly use the basic knowledge you get in those classes in some way. For example, even if you aren't cataloging resources yourself, you will be looking in your online catalog to help users all the time, and you'll have a better understanding of what you're looking at if you have taken a cataloging class. It's also important for you to have a basic understanding of the principles and terminology of librarianship so you can communicate effectively with other librarians and library staff, not only while you're interviewing but also after you've found a job and need to work collaboratively with coworkers with different types of jobs.

In addition to the required core classes, you'll need to take a bunch of electives to earn the necessary credit hours. Spend some time looking through the course offerings and see what sounds interesting as well as what's specifically relevant to what you want to do after you graduate. Take "what you want to do after you graduate" with a grain of salt, however. Many students enter library school being absolutely positive that they want to be X or Y kind of librarian when they graduate, but then they end up doing something completely different because they discover they don't like X or Y but Z is kind of fun, or they can't find a job in X or Y and have to do Q instead. (Think back to your undergrad days and remember how many of your friends were sure they were going to go to medical school. Now think about how many of them actually became doctors.) Specializing while you're in school is great, but it's also important to be a generalist. If you're sure you want to be a collections conservator, by all means take all the preservation and conservation classes your school offers, but also study other subjects.

It's okay to take courses that seem like they won't be directly relevant to your career goals. Graduate programs require you to take electives so you'll have the opportunity to explore various aspects of the profession. It's all right to take a class that doesn't seem related to what you want to do just because you love the professor or because it sounds fun. Sometimes, especially if you're working full time while you go to school and are trying to fit classes around your schedule, you may even have to take a class simply because it's offered at a convenient time. You never know when something you learned in what seemed like a random elective will come in handy, and sometimes you will surprise yourself by discovering you love a subject you took only because you needed the credit hours. As an information professional, practically nothing you ever learn will be a waste of time, so take advantage of the opportunity to learn a little bit about a lot of things while you're in school.

Take electives outside the library school if you can. Classes in human resources, business, management, budgeting, foreign languages, computer science, education, organizational psychology, and all kinds of other subjects could be extremely useful to you in your career, and they may also make you stand out from other recent graduates when you apply for jobs. It's also important to take a balance of library science and information science courses. Many library schools have names like "School of Information and Library Science" and offer degrees in information science or in library science. There is a reason these two fields are usually combined into a single graduate school, or even into a single degree (MLIS or MILS). We're more alike than we are different. As you're looking through the course catalog, don't limit yourself only to classes in the library science track or the information science track. Taking a mixture of library and information science courses will give you a better understanding of the whole profession and help you prepare to adapt to a changing marketplace. Graduating with a solid technology background makes you a more viable candidate for a variety of information jobs.

DO GRADES MATTER?

Well . . . yes and no, but mostly, no. Yes, that's probably a little simplistic, and we certainly aren't encouraging you to get bad grades. The truth is, most employers don't care about your grades unless they were really, really bad, like "barely scraped by" bad. In fact, most employers probably won't ever know how your grades were unless you tell them. They may ask for a copy of your transcript before you interview or before an offer is extended, but that's really to make sure you actually graduated from the place you said you did, not to see whether you got As or Ds. "Few employers even see a transcript," said Blanche Woolls (San José State University). "It is needed to confirm graduation but it usually resides in human resources. The abbreviations for the titles of classes are often difficult to interpret."

When you graduate from library school and enter the job market, your practical experience will be much, much more important than your grades. Getting straight As is nice, but an employer who is looking for a children's librarian will be more impressed by somebody who worked two semesters in a school library than by somebody who was a permanent fixture on the dean's list but has only read about children in books. This is not to say that it's okay to coast through with Cs and Ds, but if it comes down to getting perfect grades while not working or getting decent grades while working a series of library-related jobs and internships, *work*!

By the way, in grad school, if your program or professor allows a grade of "Incomplete," it's all right to take an Incomplete and finish the coursework later (say, the following semester). It's usually not as big a deal as it was as an undergraduate. Faculty members understand that grad students may be juggling school, work, and family obligations, so don't despair if you have to take an Incomplete; just be sure to complete that unfinished coursework as quickly as you can. In some programs, a time limit is placed on completion and failure to finish the course defaults to a failing grade.

When you enter your graduate program, you'll be assigned a faculty advisor. The school may try to match you with someone based on your career interests, or you may be paired up with someone at random. You may change advisors midway through your program because your interests have changed. It's important to develop a solid working relationship with your academic advisor. He or she will be a great source for advice and information, as well as being able to help you make decisions about which courses to take and find what job opportunities are available. Your advisor may also be a good reference for you when you enter the job market. Develop a good relationship with your advisor and make sure you meet with him or her regularly.

SHOULD I WRITE A MASTER'S PAPER/THESIS? WHAT SHOULD I WRITE ABOUT?

At your school, a master's paper or thesis may be required or optional. Writing a thesis can be intimidating, and you may have trouble thinking of something you want to write about. However, a thesis can have career benefits down the road.

If you decide to write a thesis (or don't have a choice), try to make it a valuable experience that relates to your career goals rather than a throwaway project or an obligatory hoop you're jumping through. What are you interested in? What have you heard about in your classes or experienced in your job that you want to know more about? What is relevant to your career goals? Researching the literature on a topic, doing original qualitative or quantitative research, and writing a lengthy scholarly paper can be rewarding and, especially if you're going into academic librarianship, can help you understand the research process the faculty and grad students you will serve are going through. Writing on a topic that interests you can also help you begin building a professional "brand" around a specific area of expertise. Some students are even able to get their master's papers or theses published (often with some revision), which looks fantastic on a resume when applying for jobs.

It's great if you can find something to write about that relates to your career plans, but don't feel pigeonholed or obligated to write about that subject. For example, if you want to work in collection development, it's fine to write about technology. If you want to be a systems librarian, you can still write about job satisfaction. You will probably be paired with a thesis advisor based on the subject you are writing about. Your thesis advisor may or may not be the same person as your academic advisor. You aren't cheating on your academic advisor if you pick someone else to work with you on your thesis.

If you're going into academic librarianship, you may end up working at a college or university where librarians have faculty status and tenure. If so, you will probably be required to write and do research as part of the promotion and review process. Writing a thesis in grad school is a great way to learn how to do this kind of work, and it's especially valuable to learn the ropes with a faculty advisor whose job is to help you find your way. You may not have this kind of support when you're expected to get involved in research and publishing as a librarian, so take advantage of it while you can.

CONCLUSION

Deciding where you want to earn your MLS is just the beginning of your graduate school experience. As you choose your courses and write your master's paper or thesis, keep your career goals in mind. Try to balance your required core courses with electives that give you a well-rounded view of library and information science but also allow for some specialization.

CHAPTER 3

Practical Experience

A job. I've never had a job. I don't know the first thing about having a job. All I've got on my resume is academic achievements, which will mean doodly-squat when I'm in line with eleven thousand people vying for an opening in the gardening department at Walmart.

Gilmore Girls, 2000

What could be more important than having that MLS in your hand? Well, while that degree is an essential requirement for most library jobs, it's even more important for you to get practical, hands-on, relevant work experience. Gaining relevant work experience while you're in school is probably the most important thing you can do to improve your chances of being hired as a new graduate. As Clint Chamberlain said,

To be honest, the lack of knowledge and experience that some recently-minted MLS grads bring to the table is shocking. It seems as though some students emerge from their graduate programs with little idea of what day-to-day life in a library setting is like. Students who have some kind of library work experience will rise to the top of the resume heap when applying for jobs. The experience need not be full-time; extensive volunteer work, part-time employment, internships, and other kinds of experience in the workplace are invaluable in helping job applicants set themselves apart.

WHY IS WORK EXPERIENCE SO IMPORTANT?

Without work experience, you enter the job market with the bare minimum requirement, your degree. You're competing with experienced librarians as well as with new graduates. That practical experience is what will catch the employer's attention and help you stand out. "Get a job doing something similar to what you want to do with your LIS degree, and excel at that job," said Aaron Dobbs (Shippensburg University of Pennsylvania). "With the work experience (and references) from that job, you will be more attractive to search committees." Having relevant experience allows you to tell a potential employer "I took courses on cataloging and worked on this specific cataloging project in this library" instead of merely "I took a course on cataloging."

Not only might this experience improve your chances of being hired, but it will also help you gain knowledge that will benefit you in future jobs. This practical knowledge also makes your classes more meaningful, as you relate your work experiences to your class discussions. You will often learn more on the job than you do at school, though both work together to enhance your understanding and appreciation for the field.

"Get practical hands-on experience, as much as you can," said Samantha Schmehl Hines (University of Montana). "Become well-rounded in libraries, as you never know where you may end up or what you may do in this economy."

As you gain this experience, you will learn what you like doing and what you don't like doing. This can help you shape your career goals. Let's say you enter library school thinking you'd like to be a school librarian. What happens if you graduate and take a school librarian position, only to find that you despise classroom management? If you were to work or volunteer in a school library before entering library school, or while you are in school, you might discover this and shift your career goals. For example, perhaps you'd decide that you love working with children in a public library environment instead of in a school system.

Of course, this process of learning what you like and dislike doesn't end when you graduate. Throughout your lifetime you will continue to learn more about yourself, and your personal and professional goals will shift as your likes, dislikes, situational needs, family demands, and personal priorities change over time.

"Even if you are currently working in a library, step outside that known job environment and 'try on' different work via internships, volunteering, networking, and participating in associations," said Jane Fisher (San José State University). "Get to know folks in the field, but also learn what the field is really like. See what kinds of settings and work fit well with who you are and what you can do."

Be cautious, though, when you're evaluating what you like and dislike in a job, that you stop to think about whether you like or dislike the activity or where you're doing it and who you're working with. You might find that you would love a certain type of task if you could only do it in a different work environment, or it may be that the people you're working with are so much fun that you haven't realized you don't actually enjoy what you're doing.

You'll also learn about workplace politics and appropriate professional behavior. Even if you have extensive work experience in a different field, you will learn about the way libraries (or any other information organization you end up in) work. You'll gain insight into interpersonal relationships, professional development opportunities, and challenges.

Working in the library field helps you develop your professional network. Working alongside library and information science professionals while you are a student puts you at a great advantage. For one thing, your coworkers will often be a support system for you, providing advice and resources for your coursework, career options, and job hunt. Library employers may allow you to attend some professional meetings or conferences, possibly even with some workplace funding. We'll talk more about networking in the next chapter.

FULL TIME VERSUS PART TIME

Many students wonder whether they should attend school full time to finish more quickly. Should you quit a job to attend school full time? If you work, should you work full time or part time? How many classes should you take? Of course your decision will be based mostly on your financial situation, but there are a few other factors to consider.

Obviously, attending school full time helps you earn your degree more quickly. If you decide to take a full course load, try to find a way to work part time. As we said earlier, that practical experience is as important as the degree. Some people find it difficult to handle a full course load along with a part-time job. You have to make that call for yourself, but if you find your load too heavy, consider taking a lighter course load so that you can fit that part-time work into your schedule. This may prove more helpful in the long run than rushing to earn a degree without gaining relevant work experience.

If you have a library job before you enter school, don't quit that job to attend school full time unless you find it absolutely necessary. Consider scaling back your hours at work if you can afford it, perhaps working part time while taking a partial or full load of classes. Talk with your employer about your options at work. Maybe there is a position opening up that would permit you more schedule flexibility or would allow you to learn a different set of skills. Maybe your employer could work out a more flexible schedule for your current position or could reduce your hours.

If you already have extensive library experience before entering school, you could consider making more drastic changes such as volunteering or substituting at a library while you take classes. The fact that you already have library-related work to put on your resume when you graduate may afford you more flexibility while you're in school.

If you're working outside the library field altogether and are considering a career switch into librarianship, try volunteering first. Volunteer at a library or information organization that you think would interest you. Chris Nolan said, "It lets the candidate see what they think of that type of work, and it provides an opportunity for professionals to comment on the person's work habits." Volunteer at more than one type of organization, if you can manage it. Try this out for a limited time period, perhaps one evening per week for a semester, or a certain number of hours per week for six months to a year. See how you feel about the field before you commit to a degree program. Then, if you decide you really do want to earn an MLS, look for a paid position in the field to continue to gain experience while you're in school.

SHORT TERM VERSUS LONG TERM

Should you try to work at a variety of short-term positions or take a single long-term job that lasts your entire student career? Your individual situation will determine this more than anything else. If you have a good, solid library position, and you like it, by all means, keep it. If you're looking for a change, then consider applying for a different job, perhaps one that offers new responsibilities or a better schedule. In general, prospective employers view a long-term job more positively than several short-term jobs. While you can gain more varied skills through short-term jobs, you also run the risk of being viewed as a job hopper. Employers may wonder if you were a problem employee, even if it was your choice to change jobs often. Employers view long-term employment as a sign of stability. However, extremely long-term employment in one position can lead to stagnation. Employers typically understand that student years are a time for learning and experimentation, and they view job hopping at that stage less suspiciously than they do when they see a seasoned professional doing it. If you're going to try out various types of work, this is a good time to do it. In your cover letter and resume, you can explain that you have been intentionally gaining a variety of library experiences.

STUDENT EMPLOYMENT

Several types of jobs are typically available to library school students. The type of job that's best for you will depend on your experience, the libraries and organizations in the area, how many hours per week you want to work, and, of course, what's available at the time.

Paraprofessional Positions

One of the most popular choices is a library assistant position at any type of library. These jobs may be full time or part time, may offer benefits such as insurance and paid time off, and are often good learning experiences with a great deal of responsibility. Library assistants are sometimes able to serve on committees and attend professional meetings, and they typically work side-by-side with professional librarians, often performing many of the same tasks. Unlike many other jobs on this list, paraprofessional positions are not primarily held by students. Many people take great pride in their library paraprofessional work, so don't belittle the position, even if you view it as a stepping stone in your career.

Information Jobs

If you are interested in working outside of traditional libraries after graduation, look more widely at job listings to find positions at almost any type of organization. If possible, look for organizations in a field that interests you (for example, healthcare, engineering, and so on) to gain relevant experience and develop contacts.

Student Employee Positions

Academic libraries in particular often employ students to do tasks such as shelving books. A student worker typically works fewer hours for lower wages than a library assistant and is usually not eligible for benefits. You would typically not be exposed to as much professional experience, but you might have more scheduling flexibility.

Graduate Assistantships

Schools typically have a few paid graduate assistant positions. Graduate assistants might work with faculty members, conduct research, teach classes, or work in the administrative offices, computer labs, libraries, or other areas. Some schools have more elaborate graduate assistantship programs that combine work with academics and other activities: for example, all the students in the program may meet periodically to discuss their experiences at their different work environments, or guest speakers may be invited to speak to students involved in the program.

Internships

These short-term positions can be paid or unpaid. Some can be for course credit. "Take advantage of internships to gain practical experience while in school," urged Terrie Wheeler (National Institutes of Health Library).

> If your school allows you to do this for credit, great! If not, do these internships anyway. They give you practical experience, enable you to think more critically about processes and outcomes, and provide you with professional references who can identify your strengths and possibly even assist you in finding that first job.

Field Experiences

Often your library program will require you to get some kind of limited field experience for course credit: for example, you may need to work at a reference desk for two weeks as a requirement for a reference course. You may also be expected to write a paper about your experience or to do research and write a paper about something related to the work you've done.

Use your practicum, internship, or other field experience to gain as much practical experience as you can. Employers typically do not regard these short-term experiences as highly as they do a long-term job or volunteer position, but any experience is beneficial. Field experience can be a great way to gain exposure to various types of work and to make professional contacts, and it can be effective when combined with other types of work experience.

"A lot of libraries welcome MLS students for informational visits. Take advantage of this; call libraries for an informational meeting," suggested Rosa Liu.

> What you learn at school is quite different than what you will be doing when you start working. Some MLS students have library experience on their resumes; these have a more realistic outlook as they know the library environment and enter the program knowing what to expect. I recommend highly that students with no work experience do volunteer jobs in a library that interests them.

VOLUNTEER WORK

If you can't get a paid position, or if you want exposure to an area you're not able to experience in your paid position, consider volunteering. Volunteering "shows initiative and willingness to make an extra effort to gain skills and knowledge outside the classroom," said Susan Davis.

For example, let's say you work in an academic library but you wonder if you'd like working at a public library. Volunteer at a public library to see what it's really like. Although volunteer positions are unpaid, they can provide valuable experience, insights, and networking opportunities. Volunteering "shows a willingness to dedicate yourself to the profession and gain some hands-on experience," said Jill Emery.

Volunteer work does not have to be a huge time commitment: you might volunteer a few hours on a weekend or one evening a week. You might also consider volunteering at one library for a short time (a semester or a year) and then volunteering at a different library, or a different department within the same library, to get different types of experience.

"If they're interested in working in a school library, I would tell them to volunteer in a school library, even if it's for only a few hours during the week," said Alma Ramos-McDermott (Pollard Middle School). "It's important to see how it's run, and get student/teacher interaction. What makes the candidate stand out, especially if up against candidates with experience, is that they have done something in their chosen field, even if it was an internship or volunteer role."

Ann Marie Maloney (Galen School of Nursing) advised, "Volunteer at a library or as a member of your local library advisory board. I did this and learned a great deal about public libraries I did not learn in school. Friends of the Library volunteer groups are also great places to learn and get experience."

"Volunteer to tutor students in reading, initiate a book drive, organize a library-centered workshop or conference," Judine Slaughter said. "These are things which tell the employer you enjoy working with the community in literacy so much you would do it for no pay."

MAKING THE MOST OF A LIBRARY JOB
YOU ALREADY HAVE

As we mentioned earlier, if you have a library job, hold onto it, especially in a rough economy. There are things you can do to get more out of your existing job and to gain new kinds of experiences that will appeal to future employers. If you're proactive, you can gain many of the benefits of working in a series of varied jobs without the uncertainty and risks of having to quit your paying job.

Librarians are usually happy to help fellow employees who are studying library science. Tap into the contacts and resources available in your workplace. Let the librarians you work with know that you're working on your MLS and tell them what kinds of jobs you're interested in. Not only will many of them offer to share their advice and expertise, but they'll also be more likely to put you in touch with other people they know who may be able to help you build your career.

Try to broaden your responsibilities and gain new experiences where you work. Ask your supervisor if there are opportunities for you to take on additional responsibilities that would allow you to learn something new. You might be able to work a few hours in a different department or help with a special project. Some workplaces might even allow some job sharing or swapping. For example, perhaps you work in the public services department at a large academic library; you could ask if you might be able to help with simple technical services tasks to gain exposure to a different area of your library. Most libraries have a number of projects on hold that they would gladly assign to someone who has some time to dedicate to them. When accepting special projects, though, try to find work that will teach you new skills or expand your knowledge of the field. While sticking barcodes on dusty old periodical issues is important, it may not be the best way for you to learn about developments and trends in the profession.

If you can't work in another area during your scheduled work time, consider volunteering a few hours in various areas to expand your understanding of how different departments work. Of course, you are already juggling a busy schedule with your paid job, school, and personal commitments. You don't have to volunteer a lot of hours; even a couple hours per week can give you insights into various types of library work and allow you to gain more skills and experience.

If you work in a smaller library or organization, you may already do a little of everything. Small libraries can offer wonderful learning opportunities for a library science student or new librarian. Use this opportunity to learn as much as you can about every aspect of your workplace. For example, if you work at the circulation desk in a small library, maybe you could help answer reference questions, or perhaps your supervisor would be willing to teach you more about collection development or budget management.

Consider volunteering for short-term projects or committees at your library or organization. This could allow you to learn new things and to work closely with people that you might not work with in your daily routine. Look at committees and projects outside of your library (for example, in your university, hospital, corporation, etc.)

You may decide to apply for a different paraprofessional job within your organization. Sometimes it's easier to make a lateral move into a different position or department within your organization while you are a library assistant or student employee than it is to change types of work after graduation. Moving into a different area while you're a student can provide you new experience and skills that you can list on your resume. For example, you might find a part-time position in your library that works well with your class schedule. You might move into a branch library, a different type of department, or a position with more supervisory responsibilities. Look for opportunities to add varied experience and skills while you are still a student.

In addition to varying your responsibilities, also work to gain deeper responsibility. Ask your supervisor more questions about how things work in your department. Express interest in taking on additional responsibility within your area. Maybe you can manage a short-term project or a special event. Perhaps you could work with librarians in your department to learn more about their responsibilities. As you're doing the work, think about how it relates to the things you've been learning about in class, and spend some time looking at professional literature to see what kind of research is being done on these topics and what people in the profession are saying about them.

As you take on new and varied responsibilities, be cautious that you don't overcommit yourself. It's easy to get excited about the new projects and people you're encountering. It's also very easy to accept too many new tasks. Don't neglect your primary work, what you were hired to do, in order to gain all this new experience. Initiative and ambition are highly regarded, but don't alienate your supervisors and coworkers by acting like you aren't interested in the job you're being paid to do. You'll end up struggling to get positive job references from the people who worked with you.

You may wonder if you will be able to get a professional job at a workplace where you have worked as a library assistant or student employee. This question has no easy answer. If you have established a good professional reputation at your workplace, you will stand a better chance of being considered for a professional position. However, each organization has its own organizational culture. Some prefer not to hire paraprofessionals into professional positions, while others may regularly promote from within the organization. Some people find it's difficult to shake an image as "the student" or "the paraprofessional" in an organization, no matter how much farther they go within the organization after finishing library school. Other times, though, people within an organization take pride in watching "one of their own" do great things and climb the ladder. Ask your fellow employees what the typical practice has been at your institution. No matter what they say, don't be afraid to apply.

NON-LIBRARY WORK

What if you can't find a library job? Perhaps you work in a job outside the information field and can't quit due to personal or family obligations. Maybe you're about to graduate and wonder if it's too late. All is not lost, but you will have to work extra hard to compete with applicants who have gained more relevant experience.

Look for tasks at your job that involve information management. Are there responsibilities that mirror tasks that are typically done in libraries? Your resume and cover letter should emphasize transferable skills you have gained. Transferable skills might include customer service, personnel management, budgeting, data management, and so on.

You may not wish to work in a traditional library job. Look at job ads in a wide variety of publications to find potential jobs inside and outside of traditional library environments. What skills do these job ads require? Can you develop these skills in your current job? Perhaps you can combine your MLS with your previous degrees and experience to find new roles within your current field.

CONCLUSION

Gaining practical, relevant experience is one of the most important things you can do to help yourself get hired after graduation. "I was told by one supervisor that I was offered the job partly because he was impressed by the variety of ways I had found to put myself in library service while I sought a professional position, including volunteering, as this showed a passion for the profession instead of desperation for a job," said Megan Esseltine (Westland Public Library).

It's as important to plan your practical experience gathering as it is to plan your coursework. Consciously gain skills through practical experience while you're earning your degree, so that you will enter the job market as a more competitive applicant.

CHAPTER 4

Your Professional Identity

In the end, life and business are about human connections.

The Office, 2007

Even if you're still a student, you can already begin to establish your professional identity. You can start developing a network of contacts in the field, form relationships with a few good mentors, and establish a professional online presence. You'll continue these activities throughout your career, and it will help you to start now.

NETWORKING

Networking is a popular buzzword, but what does it really mean? Do you have to walk around handing out business cards to everyone you meet? Does it involve a lot of insincere schmoozing? "Networking is building long-term professional relationships that will become a sustaining professional community," said Kim Dority. It's really just about making friends. The people you meet now, in school, on the job, even outside the library world, can all become part of your network. By nurturing those contacts you continue to expand your network. These people may provide support, advice, mentoring, job leads, ideas, opportunities to collaborate, and friendship. Of course, it's not all about what you can get; you should also offer those things to others.

The library world is a surprisingly small one, and you will come in contact with the same people repeatedly throughout your career. You'll also meet people who know the people you know. It's important to build and maintain a good professional reputation as you establish your identity in the library field.

Building a wide network of contacts is one of the most beneficial things you can do for your career and your sanity. You'll develop a support system. You can turn to your contacts for advice and ideas. Facing a problem at work? Bounce ideas off your contacts, or ask them for their suggestions. Whatever situation you're facing, someone else has dealt with it before. Are you job hunting? Spread the word among your contacts and ask them to alert you about job openings. Your contacts may be willing to serve as references on your resume. They can encourage you when you're frustrated or discouraged. You may also find people who would like to collaborate with you on a presentation, publication, or special project. Having a strong community also helps you help others; you may be able to connect others to professional opportunities.

HOW CAN I NETWORK?

At School

While you're in school, you're probably making friends with classmates and professors. Keep in touch with those friends after graduation; it's likely you'll find that some of them remain in your professional network throughout your entire career. While you're in school, look for ways to meet more of your fellow students and professors. Participate in student groups, write for student publications, or attend social activities.

If you're an online student, it's harder to connect with your fellow students and professors. You will have to make a much more dedicated effort to correspond with classmates by email. Use social networking tools and online groups to try to meet and bond with others in your program.

At Work

You'll make numerous professional contacts through your job, internship, practicum, or field experience. As you meet and work with various people, cultivate genuine friendships and keep in touch with those people after you have moved on. Get to know the people you work with. Find out what different people do. Learn who makes things happen and how information is shared in the organization. Coworkers will usually be happy to share information with you, especially while you're a student.

If you have time and your supervisor is amenable, volunteer to serve on committees or help with special projects. This allows you to meet people you might not meet otherwise in your daily activities. You can work with a wider variety of people and gain experience that you might not get through your regular position. Even if you can't officially serve on a committee—for example, if you are an intern or student employee—ask if you could sit in on a meeting or help out in some way. Again, this allows you to learn more about how things work in the real world and exposes you to new people. You can learn by observing; by watching others lead meetings, you will learn what works and what doesn't.

Network outside your immediate department or library, if possible; expand your network to the broader organization. Also consider networking outside the information science world altogether. Get your information skills out into the community or into your social circle. You may be able to help someone and perhaps even find a potential job or project.

In Professional Associations

Many students are aware of professional associations, such as the American Library Association or state or local groups, but think that they have nothing to offer these organizations while they're still in school. Others are intimidated by their size or complexity. It's important to realize that most associations offer reduced membership rates for students. Joining will allow you to get the organization's publications and learn more about the field.

Don't stop at merely joining; volunteer to participate on a committee or two. Most new graduates list a few professional memberships on their resumes, but very few have participated actively in any way. Doing so can help you stand out in pool of job applicants. Volunteering in some way at a job, in an association, or at a program shows initiative and willingness to help. You'll gain invaluable experience, and more important, you'll begin to develop friends in the library world. These are people you will come in contact with repeatedly throughout your career. Kathryn Ray (American University) said, "Every library job I've gotten in my 30-plus years of work has been because of contacts I made through the local library association. I think the best single action a new graduate can take is to become actively involved in a library association."

Participating on professional committees allows you to meet more people and expand your network beyond school and work. It also gives you a chance to do things you can't do at work; for example, perhaps you can supervise others, manage a budget, build a Web site, or plan a program. Volunteering to serve as secretary or take notes at meetings gets you face time with key people. Offering to help with a membership committee can help you meet almost everyone in the organization.

Breaking into a group, especially national associations' more sought-after committees, can be difficult. Start small. Look at student groups on campus as well as local, state, regional, and specialized library associations. Also look for groups that focus on new members. The American Library Association and many state library associations have new members' groups that typically offer a wide variety of committees designed specifically for new members. Opportunities like these give you a chance to begin your professional involvement, learn more about how the broader organization works, gain experience working on professional committees, and build your network. Once you've established a reputation as a doer, you'll often be approached when other committees have openings.

This experience benefits you in so many ways; you expand your professional network, gain more diverse experience, and build a reputation as someone who gets things done. You can use this experience and these contacts on your resume and in your job search. Professional involvement can give you an enormous lead over job applicants who have not participated at this level.

"Join associations (the student rate is generally much more affordable), attend meetings, volunteer in your associations, et cetera," said Tom Rink (Northeastern State University). "Just having a membership to an association on your resume doesn't nearly go as far as some leadership or volunteer experience with the same association. Knowing people and having them know you and your capabilities will go a long way."

When getting involved with professional associations and their committees, don't bite off more than you can chew. Begin by joining one or two groups and see what the workload is like before you accept further appointments. Earning a reputation as someone who doesn't meet your commitments or who is difficult to track down can hurt you in the long run.

Many students and new professionals think they can't get involved with professional organizations because they can't afford the expenses of traveling to conferences. While some committee appointments and other commitments do require in-person attendance at meetings, more and more groups do much of their work electronically throughout the year. When you volunteer, look for committees that involve virtual members. Even if a group doesn't explicitly mention on its Web site that it accepts virtual participation, you can always contact the chair and ask if there are ways you can participate without traveling. Express your interest in the group and why you're interested in it, and explain that although you can't attend conferences or can only attend ones within a specific region, you'd still like to work with them if possible. Many committee chairs will find a way to make things work if they're approached by highly motivated volunteers. Finally, ask colleagues to recommend committees that involve virtual members or do their work online.

YOUR ONLINE IDENTITY

Speaking of the online world, the Internet provides a critical way for you to build your professional identity. Many venues for online activity are available, from more traditional mailing lists and bulletin boards to the ever-evolving world of social media, including Facebook, blogs, and Twitter. Online activity can be informative, network-building, stress-busting, and just plain fun. At the same time, you should be cognizant of the way you're presenting yourself online, particularly when you're hunting for jobs.

You can use the Internet in many ways to your advantage as you're beginning to build your career and develop your professional identity. Look for mailing lists and discussion forums related to the types of libraries or areas of specialization that interest you.

When you subscribe and begin to follow the conversation, give yourself time to watch the discussion and develop a sense of tone and protocol. Sometimes students make the mistake of joining a mailing list and immediately charging out of the gate with guns blazing. They unleash a furious barrage of questions and opinions and often quickly burn out supernova style. This behavior sticks in people's minds and can come back to hurt you if they later see your application show up in a candidate pool. That's not to say you can't participate in discussions on mailing lists or forums; on the contrary, it's good to get involved and to ask questions in a restrained, thoughtful way. Just as people remember the names of mailing list pests, they also remember the names of posters who ask good questions and offer insightful comments. You don't have to be an expert on everything to participate in the discussion; just think before you post and ask yourself whether what you're saying is adding to the conversation.

Some people wonder about the role social media plays in job searching and identity building. How can you balance your personal Facebook, blog, and Twitter use with your professional use? Common sense is the key. When posting anything online in a forum that's publically accessible, ask yourself, "Would I want potential employers to see this?" This does not mean that you can't have a personal life on the Internet. Working professionals, including the ones who may interview you when you graduate, have personal lives, too. They have friends, pets, children, and hobbies; they go on vacation and to parties; they can be silly and irreverent. They don't expect you to be some kind of 24-7 library robot. Just remember that whatever you put up on the Internet with your name on it may be seen by potential employers and it may affect the opinion they develop of you. A good rule of thumb is that if it's something you wouldn't want your mother to see or hear about, you probably don't want potential employers to see or hear about it either. A photo that shows you riding a roller coaster with your friends is fine; a photo of you passed out on the floor at a conference reception is problematic. Use privacy settings on social media sites wisely.

The worst misuse of the Internet, however, and the one that may send your applications to the "no" pile the fastest, is complaining about your bosses, instructors, or colleagues, including fellow students. Don't use your publicly viewable Twitter feed or blog to talk about what a jerk your boss is, how incompetent the people you work with are, and how stupid everybody but you is. This goes for discussion lists, too; don't use them to trash your colleagues. Similarly, don't broadcast to the world how you spent eight hours at work yesterday goofing off or how boring and pointless your jobs and classes are. The last thing you want to do is to use the Internet to tell the world that you are irresponsible, difficult, disgruntled, lazy, or troublemaking.

Use the Internet to your advantage by building a positive online presence. Ask smart questions, make valuable comments, and network with those you know and those you'd like to know. Use mailing lists, discussion forums, and social media like Twitter, Facebook, and LinkedIn to learn, keep in touch with your professional network, and let them know what you've been doing.

MENTORING

Building a wide network of contacts as your career grows is an essential part of your professional development. Many of these contacts will be somewhat casual, such as people you've worked with on a single project, met in a workshop, or even struck up a conversation with on a shuttle bus at a conference. At the same time, it's important to develop more substantial long-term relationships with people in the profession who can watch your career develop, give you advice, help you make long-range plans for your future, and tell you when you're heading down the wrong road. A mentor can serve all these roles and more.

As a whole, librarians are helpful; it's a character trait that leads many to the profession in the first place. This means it's likely you'll meet many people who are happy to give you advice on your career whether you asked for it or not. Often the best advice, however, comes from people who have known you for a long time, have watched you build your career over an extended period, and who understand your strengths and weaknesses. In her article "Mentor Match-ups," Kim Dority wrote, "Choose a mentor who *gets you.* A mentor's job is not to *change* who you are, but to understand who you are and help you learn or devise ways to minimize the impact of your weaknesses and maximize that of your strengths." Finding one or more mentors early in your career can build this connection and help you find your way in the profession.

Some library schools and professional associations have formal mentoring programs that match students or recent graduates with more experienced professionals who have expressed an interest in serving in such a role and are therefore committed to a long-term expenditure of time and effort. Mentoring relationships can also begin accidentally or serendipitously. Students who are working in an internship, field experience, paraprofessional position, or part-time job are often drawn to more established colleagues who share an interest and have compatible personalities. Look for people you respect and admire and whom you'd like to model your career after, and ask them questions. Their responses will give you an idea of whether they'd be amenable to serving as a mentor to you in the long run. Don't take it personally if it takes you a while to find a mentor; it's a big commitment of time and energy and some people will be too busy, while others may feel that they aren't settled or established enough in the profession themselves yet to serve as a mentor to others.

Sometimes students and new professionals are drawn to their supervisors as mentors. Your boss will probably be the person you spend the most time with and may be working in the type of job or environment you'd like to work in, so convenience may lead you to consider him or her a mentor. Sometimes supervisors can and do serve as excellent mentors. Use caution, however, because the supervisor-employee relationship is already a tricky one, and viewing your boss as a mentor will make things even more complicated. A mentor needs to be someone who will be honest with you, even when he or she is saying something you don't want to hear, and it may be awkward to hear these messages coming from the person who also writes your performance reviews. You may also want to use your mentor as someone to give you advice on how to work successfully with your supervisor; obviously this won't fly if your mentor and your boss are the same person. This is not to say that your boss can't be a good mentor, but you shouldn't automatically gravitate to him or her without considering others in your department or library. You may also find that you can develop a mentoring relationship with a supervisor after you've moved on to a different position and are no longer reporting to him or her.

"I would strongly recommend asking for a mentor," Amber Conger (Richland County Public Library) said.

> When I started my new job, there were so many things I wanted to know about but didn't want to ask for fear of being viewed as gossiping. Now I have a person to bounce all of my questions off of, and she shares her wisdom with me (saving my sanity on more than one occasion!). I am learning from someone who is truly diplomatic and well-respected, and I feel that I can trust her advice and experience.

Mentors will serve many important roles as you begin to find your way in the profession. They will answer your questions, introduce you to other people, give you advice, help you navigate tricky waters, give you a pep talk when you're feeling down, provide a reality check when you're feeling sorry for yourself, and help you celebrate your successes and learn from your failures. Your mentor should be someone who can be honest with you without hurting your feelings, and also who will give you constructive criticism when you're making bad choices or going down the wrong path.

Remember that being your mentor is not this person's full-time job. Be respectful of his or her time and be flexible. While mentors also get something out of the relationship—personal satisfaction, a sense of giving back to the profession, a feeling of being a proud parent without having to give birth to you or endure your teenage years—remember that they're doing something they don't have to do. Be understanding when your mentor has to reschedule meetings with you or is occasionally too busy to give you much time.

Keep in mind that sometimes mentoring relationships just don't work out. If your mentor is consistently unavailable or chronically canceling appointments with you, it may be that he or she isn't willing or able to mentor you any longer. Be honest with each other and keep in mind that most mentoring relationships reach an end eventually. Remember what worked and didn't work, and what you found particularly useful, so you can serve as a good mentor to others later in your career.

CONCLUSION

Networking is not a four-letter word; it's a critical part of your professional development. To be successful in any profession, you need to begin building a network of contacts early in your career and constantly nurture those relationships. Building connections with others inside and outside the profession will help you find jobs, get involved in projects, and answer questions, including those you didn't even know you had. The people in your network will teach, energize, and inspire you, and some of them will become your friends.

When building connections, don't think only about how others can help you. Networking is always a two-way street. Look for ways you can help others as well as being aware of how others can help you.

WORK CITED

Dority, G. Kim. "Mentor Match-ups: How to Find the One (or Two or Three)," http://infonista.com/2011/mentor-match-ups (cited February 23, 2012).

CHAPTER 5

Additional Skills

It is not our abilities that show what we truly are. It is our choices.

Harry Potter and the Chamber of Secrets, 2002

All graduates will have the same degree, and many will have some practical experience. So let's say you have an MLS and a history of relevant work. What else do employers look for on a resume? What other skills will be useful? What else can you do now to help set yourself apart from the competition in a job search?

You can add value to yourself as a candidate by doing things beyond the minimum—that is, getting your degree and some experience. Publishing and presenting are two activities that many employers value. You can also demonstrate your value by showing that you are comfortable with emerging technologies, are proficient in a foreign language, or have other specialized skills or knowledge.

PUBLISHING

Even if you never publish a thing, you will need to be able to express ideas clearly and concisely. Written communication is essential to your success in your career. If you end up in an environment where librarians have tenure, your writing could determine whether you keep your job or lose it. In a job search, strong writing skills can help set you apart from other applicants. Your writing can give potential employers an idea of your capabilities and can make you appear more invested in contributing to the profession.

If your writing skills aren't strong, consider taking a class or working with a tutor to improve them. Many colleges offer writing workshops and assistance. You might also be able to work with a friend or mentor who can evaluate your writing and give you constructive feedback.

Where Can I Publish?

If you have never written for publication before, start small. Does your library school have a student newsletter? Does your university have a student newspaper? Investigate your local library association's newsletters or other publications. If you have a job, see if you can write something for your workplace's newsletter, Web site, blog, or other publications. Perhaps you can create pamphlets or public relations materials for your organization. You can even hone your writing skills by creating written guides that will be used by your library's users. Don't limit yourself to print publications; also look into electronic publishing opportunities. Some online publications offer newer writers the opportunity to publish articles with a lower barrier to entry than traditional print publications. If you have an interest in a particular subject, consider creating a blog or Web site about it. This allows you to showcase your writing ability and build expertise in a subject area that interests you.

Think about non-refereed journals. They can often be good starting points for new writers. Also look into regular columns that publish works from guest contributors. Don't be afraid to approach a major journal, though, if you have substantive research that you would like to present. For example, if you wrote a thesis as part of your MLS, you may be able to adapt it for submission to scholarly journals. Talk to your advisor or other library school faculty to get advice on how you might pursue turning work you've already done into your first published article.

How Do I Start?

Always read the publication's guidelines for authors before you submit an idea to the editors. This holds true for any publication, whether it's as informal as LIScareer.com or as formal as *Library Quarterly*. Read several previous issues to become familiar with the content, writing style, and intended audience of the publication. This also helps you avoid duplicating topics that have already been covered, though, really, almost any topic has been covered at least once, so don't let that discourage you. To succeed, you should have a new approach to the topic.

When you're starting out, it can often be helpful to join a writing group. Members of writing groups can offer support, critique each other's work, and let each other know about publishing opportunities. Writing groups can be local, with in-person meetings, or online, with members from around the world. You might even want to consider starting a writing group; for example, you could create a writing group with fellow students who are interested in publishing.

Consider writing with a partner, if you know someone with whom you might work well. If you're new to writing, try to find an experienced writer who might be willing to coauthor an article with you; you can learn from the other writer as you work on your first publication. Don't feel you have to work with an experienced writer, though; two new writers can work well together as they help each other break into publishing.

Coauthoring has many benefits. You motivate each other and have someone to bounce ideas off of. As your interest and motivation wax and wane (and they will), your writing partner can pick up the slack and help keep you going, and vice versa. Multiple authors can provide more well-rounded coverage of a topic because each author brings a different perspective to the project. Similarly, you may find someone whose writing style complements yours well; perhaps your style is wordy and your partner's is terse, but working together you can edit each other's work and find a happy medium that flows well.

Writing with a coauthor can also have drawbacks. It's like those dreaded group projects you may have experienced in school; if one person doesn't carry his or her weight, the others will resent the added burden. If you find that your coauthor really isn't contributing, you may want to ask if he or she would like to continue to be involved; sometimes you will find that he or she would be relieved to bow out of the project. In most cases, coauthoring is a great way to write for professional publications, and it can often help you forge a relationship with a coauthor whom you'd like to work with again and again.

PRESENTING

Presenting to an audience is an important skill, especially if you plan to apply for positions in instruction, public services, children's librarianship, or management. Fear of speaking in front of groups is one of the most common fears people face. However, there are very few jobs that do not require you to speak in front of a group at least occasionally. In some cases you'll have to present information to students, clients, customers, or supervisors. If you're in a tenure-track position in an academic library, you'll be expected to give presentations or serve as a panelist at professional meetings. If you begin publishing regularly, you'll often be invited to present at workshops and conferences. Some positions require you to present in order to raise funds or support for your organization, or to serve the community. If you can list public speaking experience on your resume, you have an advantage over other applicants who don't have that background.

The presentations that you list on your resume do not need to be library-related. If you've taught any type of classes, presented at any workplace, or spoken to groups, you can often list those presentations on your resume to show that you have public speaking experience.

How Do I Improve My Presenting Skills?

As a student, you probably have to do classroom presentations occasionally. It's not appropriate to list those on your resume, but you can use those opportunities to work on your public speaking skills. You can sometimes repackage the research you did for that class project into a presentation for a professional conference.

Presenting is an acquired skill that does not come easily to most people. Consider joining a speaking group such as Toastmasters International. Work with a mentor or friend to practice presenting. Perhaps you could create a support group among fellow students or coworkers. You could also look into volunteer opportunities that would allow you to present to groups, such as leading story times for children or teaching computer skills to seniors. Public libraries often welcome this kind of volunteer assistance, but you could also gain it through non-library organizations.

Attend presentations at your school or at professional meetings, and be on the lookout for opportunities to watch free webinars. Watch other people present and think about their presentation skills. You can learn a lot by watching both good and bad presentations. What did the speakers do that worked well? What do you wish they had done differently? Did they engage the audience? Did they make eye contact, or did they spend the entire time looking down at their notes? Did they know their material well? Were they comfortable with the technology they used in their presentations? Did they make you want to sneak out of the room and not come back?

A good way to ease into public speaking at conferences is to do a poster session based on research you've done or a project you've worked on. A poster session is a bit like the science fair presentations you may have done when you were younger. You create a display (hence the "poster" part) about your research or project and stand at a table in a room with lots of others who are doing the same thing. As attendees walk through the room looking at the displays, you answer any questions they have about your work and your findings. You may also be expected to give a brief talk about your work every 10 to 15 minutes. Many people, particularly those early in their careers, find doing a poster session less stressful than doing a full-fledged presentation, because it involves standing at a table talking to individuals or small groups rather than standing at a podium speaking into a microphone in front of a room full of people. Large and small conferences, including local and regional ones, often have time set aside for poster sessions. They can be a perfect opportunity for library school students or recent graduates to gain valuable public speaking experience by talking about research or projects they did as part of their classwork.

Another way to gain experience speaking in front of others is by presenting talks at brown bag sessions. The idea behind a brown bag talk is that people bring their lunches and listen to others give brief talks about their work, research, trends in the profession, or anything else they're interested in. Ask others at your workplace if such brown bag sessions ever take place, and, if so, see if you can give a short talk at one of them. You can also organize a brown bag session with other students. Reserve a room somewhere on campus for an hour around lunchtime and find people who want to give brief talks on their jobs, articles they've read recently, or their research. Promote the brown bag session to fellow students and faculty.

Anything you can do to gain experience speaking in front of others will be beneficial. There are lots of opportunities to become more comfortable giving presentations and talking in front of a group. Many people who are terrified by that idea find that they actually enjoy it when they force themselves to do it. Public speaking is definitely one of those things that will become much easier as you do more of it, and employers want to hire people who can speak effectively and comfortably in front of a group.

TECHNOLOGY

Technology skills are essential in an information job, but acquiring the right ones can be tricky. Technology changes so quickly that what's hot now probably won't be applicable two years from now. Focus on learning concepts rather than specific software. It's important to be comfortable with technology, including computer programs, databases, presentation software, office applications, and other commonly used technology. Stay aware of the newest and emerging technology when you are preparing for a job search. When applying for jobs, it's important to show that you're comfortable keeping up with rapid changes.

"Show that you know the basics; a solid print and online resume demonstrate writing and tech skills," said Beth Doyle.

> Highlight projects you have done as a student or intern that demonstrate your ability to learn new tools and apply them to a successful project. It's important to be able to communicate how you have researched, planned, and implemented a project, and what you have learned from it: what you would do again and what you would change.

While you're in school, take technology classes and use every opportunity to become comfortable with various programs. Ask your coworkers and local librarians which tools they most commonly use and what technology skills they value. These questions can also inspire interesting and valuable conversations on discussion lists. Consider taking technology classes in non-LIS departments. In addition to for-credit technology classes, universities often offer free workshops on using popular applications to faculty, staff, and students, and you may be able to download popular software at a huge discount (or even for free!) by taking advantage of deals your school has worked out with the manufacturer. Use the software available in computer labs or online. Play around on your own, in local libraries, online, at work, at school. Take advantage of free vendor training opportunities at conferences or at work when they're available. Notice what technology skills are listed in job postings and look for ways to learn at least a little about those skills.

When it comes to technology, the more tools and applications you're exposed to, the easier it becomes to pick up new skills. Try to set goals for yourself, such as "I will get experience using one new piece of software per month." Even if you never use some of those specific tools again, you will feel less intimidated when presented with unfamiliar technology in the future and will have picked up good learning habits. Potential employers will appreciate your ability and willingness to learn about new technology.

LANGUAGE SKILLS

Familiarity with one or more foreign languages can be tremendously helpful to librarians, no matter what type of position or organization they work in. Many libraries, particularly public and school libraries, serve communities with large numbers of non-English speakers. Librarians who work in technical services, such as catalogers and acquisitions specialists, frequently deal with materials in a multitude of languages. Therefore, any knowledge you have of languages other than English will look great on your resume.

Even if you didn't study another language in school or as an undergraduate, it's not too late to pick up some basic proficiency. As we mentioned in chapter 3, you may be able to take a foreign language class as an elective while in library school. Community colleges often offer instruction in foreign languages at very reasonable rates.

If you took another language when you were younger but it's become rusty from years of disuse, you may be surprised at how easily you can regain the basics. If you can't take formal classes, you may be able to brush up on languages you've almost lost by checking out self-instruction materials from your library, finding instructional videos or exercises online, or locating people in your community who speak the language and would be willing to meet with you regularly to help refresh your skills.

Don't feel that you need to be fluent in a language for it to be useful. Any knowledge of other languages that you have will make you stand out. Frequently, particularly in technical services positions, *reading* knowledge of the language matters more than the ability to speak or understand it. Read foreign newspapers online and see how much you can understand. You don't need to know every single word, but read articles and see if you get the gist of what they're about. Being able to put "reading knowledge of Spanish" or "bibliographic knowledge of Russian" on your resume will make you stand out from many of the other applicants in the pile.

BUSINESS SKILLS

Business skills are helpful for any position, especially those with managerial responsibilities. If you've held management positions, your resume should demonstrate those skills through the descriptions you give of each job you've had. If you'd like to move into a management position but haven't had that type of experience so far, look for ways to gain supervisory skills either in your current job or in a volunteer position. Remember that you don't have to be supervising permanent, full-time staff to gain valuable experience; you can also gain great managerial skills by supervising student assistants, volunteers, or temporary workers.

It's not common to include a Management Skills or Business Skills section on a resume, but sometimes you can highlight management experience that you gained outside of your work in other ways. For example, let's say you served as president of the parent-teacher organization at your child's school or organized 400 volunteers for your local library association. You could list these positions, with a brief description of your accomplishments, under headings such as Volunteer Work, Professional Activities, or Community Service.

Keep in mind that you can gain valuable management and business skills without being someone's boss. Skills such as budgeting and publicity are also in high demand in libraries. If you gained this kind of experience in previous non-library jobs or through student organizations or activities in the community, you may be able to include them on your resume or talk about them while interviewing for a job.

CONCLUSION

As a new graduate, you will compete with other candidates who may have more experience than you. You can make yourself a stronger candidate by adding extracurricular activities or additional skills to your arsenal. Putting in the extra effort to publish articles, give presentations, and develop valuable skills will help you stand out and prompt employers to give your application a second look.

SECTION 2

The Job Search

CHAPTER 6

How Employers Hire

I tell you, this is a great country. You know what makes it great? Because you don't have to be witty or clever as long as you can hire someone who is.

The Mary Tyler Moore Show, 1977

Have you ever wondered how things work on the employer's side of a job search? What do employers do when they receive your resume? Why does it often take so long for you to hear anything? What is a search committee and what do they do? What can you do to keep yourself in the running?

To someone who has never been involved in filling a vacant position from the employer's side, the process can seem very mysterious. You may feel that you send your application materials off into a black hole and you probably wonder what happens next. This chapter will give you a sense of what employers and search committees do during a job search. As a job seeker, knowing more about the other side of the process and having reasonable expectations of what might happen next may make you feel less helpless and give you some peace of mind.

Of course, the hiring process varies depending on the type of organization. No two places run their searches exactly the same way, but most libraries and other information agencies follow similar patterns when posting a vacancy and running a search.

Often, when employers receive your resume, they will not do anything with it until the application deadline has passed. You may receive an acknowledgement that your application has been received, but that's not guaranteed. Indeed, you will find that many organizations are not very communicative. This can sometimes help you evaluate whether you'd like to work there or not! It can also just mean they're overwhelmed with huge numbers of applications.

After the deadline, the human resources officer, hiring manager, or search committee members will begin reviewing all the resumes. They typically have a checklist of required and preferred qualifications based on the job ad. First they will weed out any applicants who do not meet the basic requirements—for example, someone who will not hold the MLS by the position's start date. If the job announcement has identified certain qualifications as being required, they may be legally prohibited from considering you for the job if you don't meet them. Then they will often make several passes through the pile of resumes, comparing each candidate's qualifications to their checklist. They will continue to narrow down the pile until they have a small number of resumes left. If hiring is being done by a search committee, the members will probably each review the remaining applications and then meet as a group to discuss their impressions of each candidate in that final pile. If the hiring is done by a manager or human resources officer, that person will often consult with a supervisor or personnel within the department.

The committee or hiring officer will select a few candidates to interview. Some institutions conduct telephone interviews before bringing candidates in for in-person interviews. A few candidates are then invited for an in-person interview. Academic library interviews often last one or two days, while other employers tend to hold interviews that last about half a day.

Some employers pay the candidates' travel expenses while others don't. You may have to decide whether you are willing to pay your own way to an interview. If the employer does not pay your way, try to find out from your network if this employer is having financial problems, or if the organization typically hires locally. For example, it's common for public libraries not to pay candidates' expenses because they often hire local applicants. On the other hand, academic libraries, particularly larger ones, typically consider the pool for their positions to be nationwide, so bringing candidates in from far away is often considered a given.

Employers frequently do not tell the entire applicant pool anything about the job search until they have finished the whole process—that is, after they have offered a job and the offer has been accepted. They don't want to send you a rejection letter and then have to go back and reopen the search if their selected candidate refuses the job. This is why candidates often wait six months or longer to hear the status of an application to an academic library. Response time for public, school, special, and non-traditional employers is usually much quicker.

"Start applying to jobs during your last semester of school," urged April Pavis (Loudoun County Public Library). "You will get plenty of 'thanks but no thanks' letters, but many libraries will store your resume and may pull it up when a similar job needs filling. I was contacted for an interview for a job I applied to more than six months earlier."

THE ACADEMIC LIBRARY HIRING PROCESS

Library personnel write or update the job description, which must be approved by university administration. The library forms a search committee, which could be comprised of librarians, staff, and university faculty. After the resumes are received, the search committee reviews them.

Nancy George described the search committee's selection process at her workplace.

Using the position description as a guide, resumes are sorted, with those that contain the minimum qualifications retained. Out of those resumes that have the minimum qualifications, these are also sorted, giving preference to those resumes that appeal to the committee due to candidates' experiences and education, the cover letters, and information given in the resumes. The search committee then ranks the resumes and the top twelve or so are invited for phone interviews.

The search committee conducts telephone interviews with top candidates in order to narrow down the pool. They then invite the top few candidates to interview in person. Academic library interviews are often very long and grueling. Candidates meet with the search committee, librarians, library staff, non-library administrators, human resources personnel, and perhaps faculty over a one- to two-day interview. Candidates are sometimes required to make a presentation. Smaller academic libraries often work much more quickly. The interviews are much shorter, ranging from several hours to one day.

After interviewing all candidates, the search committee chair usually solicits comments on the candidates from library staff and others who met with them during their interviews. After reviewing those comments, the search committee members meet to discuss the candidates and write a report making a recommendation to the library director or dean. If none of the interviews went well, it's possible that the committee may recommend bringing in more candidates from the applicant pool, or even reposting the job and reopening the search. Once a recommendation is made, the university administrators may also have to approve the selection. The library director, HR manager, or dean then contacts the successful candidate with a job offer. When an offer is accepted, the search committee chair notifies the other on-campus interviewees to tell them that someone else has accepted the position. Someone in the library director's office or university human resources office typically notifies all other applicants by letter or email that the job has been filled.

The academic library search process can move very slowly. "This entire process, from job posting to closing the search, can take two months when all goes well, and up to four months if early candidates don't pan out and the search committee must return to the applicant pool," said Diane Calvin. Aaron Dobbs agreed.

The whole hiring process takes the library from eleven to forty-two months. Applicants think they have it rough waiting up to a year to hear; the library usually has been waiting for the new hire for eighteen to thirty-six months. Case in point: I was hired three years after my predecessor retired and thirteen months after I applied.

THE PUBLIC LIBRARY HIRING PROCESS

Because public libraries are city or county departments, they must follow governmental policies and procedures. Typically the librarians create or update a job description which must be approved by a government human resources officer. Some libraries require applications with no resumes, some request electronic resumes, some use paper applications only, and others may accept a combination.

"Follow the instructions!" urged Marcia Anderson (Grand Rapids Area Library).

Our city's application process is very strict, and we still require paper applications. If it says no resume, don't send one, because I won't be able to look at it when I score applications. I've had to eliminate applications with "see attached resume" in several places on the application form because the instructions clearly stated "Resumes will not be considered." Also, make sure you allow enough time for your application to arrive if you mail it. I have been disappointed when I could not consider a promising candidate whose application packet arrived the day after the posted deadline.

Applications are typically collected by the human resources department and passed on to the department head or library director. The library director reviews applications, often with another librarian, with a library human resources officer, or with a small search committee.

"At my library, the department head and another librarian typically score the applications," said Maria Pontillas (Tacoma Public Library).

When I participated in this process I was very surprised that resumes were given no weight at all and each applicant was scored solely on how they answered the supplemental questions. My advice to new grads would be to pay attention to the supplemental questions. A simple "refer to my resume" won't do. Be sure to answer each question thoroughly even though it may mean restating what's on your resume.

After applications are reviewed, a few candidates are invited for in-person interviews. Interviews typically last a few hours. The candidate usually meets with the supervisor for the vacant position and perhaps with the library director. In a small library, the candidate may meet with the entire library staff. In a larger metropolitan library system, applicants may interview at the main administrative office with the library system director, administrators, and human resources officer. If the applicant is applying for a position at a branch library, he or she will typically interview with the branch manager.

Applicants may not receive acknowledgments until the search process has closed. The decision process usually moves more quickly than in academic libraries. The library director or search committee chair makes an offer to the top candidate. If the candidate accepts, then all remaining candidates will be notified that the job has been filled.

THE SCHOOL LIBRARY HIRING PROCESS

School librarians are usually hired much like teachers. Hiring may be handled by the district's library services director or the school's principal. Some schools form a search committee that might include the principal, some teachers, and possibly some parents or students. Applications are usually received online.

Some districts use telephone interviews, then in-person interviews at the school, followed by in-person interviews with district administrators. Others interview all applicants in brief in-person interviews to narrow the field; the search committee then interviews a smaller group of applicants, and the two or three finalists then interview with district human resources personnel or administrators.

"On your resume, include any teaching experience you've had, whether it was in a classroom or library," urged Alma Ramos-McDermott. "School librarians are expected to teach. Cover letters and references are expected, and are very much used."

Kim McLean (Ann Arbor Public Schools) concurred.

I found that references were absolutely necessary and I believe having well-rounded references from school, work, and volunteer experience was what got me my job. Most of the school questions were the same: What will you do to help address the achievement gap? How will you teach to a diverse group of students (culturally, academically, etc.)?

How will you develop relationships with your students, staff and the parents? Why do you want to work here, specifically in this school in this district?

THE FEDERAL AND STATE GOVERNMENT HIRING PROCESS

"The hiring process for the federal government is one big labyrinth, but with the current hiring reforms the process is getting better," said Nancy Faget (U.S. Government Printing Office). Federal and state agencies follow standardized processes. Candidates must submit applications and all required supporting documents by the posted deadline in order for their applications to be considered. The human resources department initially screens applicants and then sends names of qualified applicants to the hiring manager. The manager then selects several candidates to interview. Telephone interviews may be used to determine whether to invite an out-of-town candidate for an in-person interview. Candidates pay their own travel expenses. "We are required to fill a position within eighty days of posting," explained Rosa Liu. "An applicant should hear within three weeks after an interview, if he or she got the job. Cover letters are not required. References are taken seriously and are checked before a candidate is considered for employment."

Dawn Krause described her state library's process: "We score the applications via a matrix that is developed along with the job description and interview questions." The committee members rank the applications and interview the top candidates. In interviews, committee members ask questions and write the candidates' answers down on their question sheets. "We go through all the questions with no back-and-forth conversation with the applicant," continued Krause. "The candidate can ask for clarification on a question but can't engage the interviewers in conversation around the topics in the questions." At the end of the question period, candidates may ask questions and meet other library staff.

After the interview, each committee member scores the candidate's answers to determine a total score. Hiring decisions are based on these scores, "so thoroughly answering each question is absolutely vital to our process," Krause explained.

The high scorer wins, basically. This process is in place to ensure that everyone has the very same experience in applying for, and interviewing for, our jobs. It also allows us to have the appropriate paperwork on file should we ever get questioned about our process. It also tries to ensure that bias or favoritism does not come into play since the scoring system determines who gets hired.

THE SPECIAL LIBRARY OR NON-LIBRARY HIRING PROCESS

The hiring process in the for-profit world differs significantly from the library environment. Applications are usually handled online, often through a generic recruiting site. The initial application review is typically handled by a human resources or talent acquisition department.

Top candidates often participate in a telephone interview before being invited to interview on site. Candidates often interview with people who have no library science expertise. A typical interview might last several hours to half a day.

Steve Oberg, who has worked for academic libraries, vendors, and for-profit organizations, said:

> For entry level jobs in the for-profit sector, I cannot stress enough how important it is that job seekers look for ways of getting their feet in the door, of getting noticed. Typically the best way to do that is to look for onsite internship opportunities. This is invaluable experience and can often result in a job offer if you give a favorable impression.

SURVIVING THE JOB SEARCH PROCESS

The job search is arduous for both employers and candidates. It's a little like dating: you're both trying to figure out if you're a good fit for each other. "Realize that it's all about 'fit' for the job and the organization in which the job exists," agreed Steve Oberg. "You may be the most qualified, but if those who interview you or review your resume don't think you provide a good fit, it doesn't matter."

While it's impossible not to be disappointed when you don't get a job you'd hoped for, try not to become too discouraged. Don't take the employer's rejection personally. Employers often receive hundreds of applications for one job opening. At times they must choose between many desirable candidates, sometimes including internal candidates whom they already know. Try to remain optimistic and enthusiastic so that you are prepared for the next interview or opportunity.

"Remember that the job search is more of an art than a science and never take rejection personally," encouraged Ava Iuliano.

> It may not have been the position that would have allowed you to thrive as a professional. Every rejection you receive is simply more information you can collect for your job search. As librarians, we often invest a large amount of our personal identity in our profession; the job search is the one time you must work to separate your identity as a professional and your personal identity.

CHAPTER 7

Your Job Search

Instead of telling our young people to plan ahead, we should tell them to plan to be surprised.

Dan in Real Life, 2007

The job search—now that's an overwhelming thought, isn't it? How do you even start looking for a job? Before you begin applying for jobs, take some time to assess your goals and organize your job search.

ASSESS YOURSELF

First, think about your skills, interests, and career goals. Consider both your preferences and your absolute requirements. You might *need* to stay in your current location because of your family. You might *prefer* to work in an academic library, but you're open to the idea of working in any type of workplace.

What background work experience and education do you have? What skills have you gained through previous jobs, hobbies, extracurricular activities, and educational experiences? What do you do well? What do you like to do? What do you dislike? How strongly do you dislike it; that is, would you prefer to spend very little time working at a reference desk, or does the thought terrify you so much that you wish you could hide under the desk? What are your career goals? Are you open to any type of job? What restrictions do you have? Are you able to move anywhere? Are you able to work a non-traditional schedule? Are you open to any type of work environment or organization?

Talk with librarians in a variety of roles so that you can learn more about what they do. You can read about career options in books such as our *A Day in the Life* or Rachel Singer Gordon's *What's the Alternative?* Kim Dority's *Rethinking Information Work* offers guidance for self-assessment and career planning.

As you assess yourself, try to stay as open-minded as you can about potential work in order to give yourself the widest range of options. You'll learn more about yourself throughout your career, and your goals will probably change over time, so don't worry if you aren't sure yet what your ideal job is.

ORGANIZE YOUR SEARCH

Job hunting is very time consuming. Treat your job search as you would a job. Set aside time each day or week to work on job hunting. Setting up a system can be helpful. For example, you might search job ads for 30 minutes every day and work on resumes one day a week. "Work in an organized way," urged Wendy Israel (Seattle Public Library). "Check the job listings a couple times a week, revise your cover letter and resume to fit that job, send it off on Friday, and take the weekend off."

Don't let yourself get overwhelmed or depressed by the hugeness of the task or the "what ifs" that you can't control. Focus your energy on preparing the best resumes and cover letters that you can.

Break tasks down into smaller steps. Begin by preparing a master list of your skills, experience, education, and other qualifications. Then use that master list to build a few basic resumes and cover letters that you can adapt fairly quickly when you see a job ad that interests you.

Set up some kind of filing system, whether it's a notebook, accordion file, or digital files on your computer. Keep track of your job search information, including various versions of your resumes and cover letters, job ads you apply for, resumes and cover letters you send, responses you've received, contact information for your references, and any other related information.

INCREASE THE ODDS

Widen your search as much as possible. Being open to almost any geographic location, type of library, type of position, and so on improves your chances of finding a job more quickly. In a tough job market, it's especially important to be flexible.

Stepping Stones

Your first job might not be your ideal job, but it can be a starting point or stepping stone to a more satisfying job. It's a little like an actor waiting tables while waiting for a big break. Don't worry too much about finding a perfect entry-level job. Find one that meets most of your criteria and use that job to gain experience that will help you in future job searches. We're not suggesting that your first job isn't important, and it's completely possible that you may find a terrific job right off the bat. It's likely that you will move on or up in a few years, so at this entry-level stage, broaden your search as much as you can so that you can get that first job.

When looking at ads, don't limit yourself to library publications or job sites. Search through local job listings and general job sites using terms such as "information," "knowledge," and "researcher" to help you find the widest variety of jobs possible. For example, Blane Dessy (Library of Congress) said, "In the federal government, MLS degree holders are also archivists, information specialists, Web managers, et cetera. Look beyond your own professional label to maximize the job opportunities."

Being geographically mobile will make your job search much easier. The wider you cast your net, the more likely you'll catch something. Many students don't want to move because they like where they're living or perhaps they give undue weight to non-essential reasons for staying where they are. Graduates have a particularly difficult time finding jobs in areas with one or more library schools. It's a buyer's market for libraries in those locations; there are far more graduates than jobs, and it's easy for employers to find librarians, including some who are willing to accept lower salaries to remain in that location.

Your first job is not forever, and it's easier to get your second job than your first one. You may find it's beneficial to move away for a few years to take a great job in what may not be your ideal location, get some strong experience under your belt, and then move to a more desirable location for your second job, possibly at a higher salary. Obviously some people aren't able to relocate due to family or other commitments, and they must widen their search in other ways. If you *can* move, keep an open mind about where you'd be willing to live for a couple of years.

Transferable Skills

Consider your transferable skills. When you read a job posting, think about how your skills match the required skills in the ad. Widen your options by considering how your previous job experience, volunteer experience, hobbies, community involvement, and so on might meet the job requirements.

"Highlight your experience, either library or non-library, that demonstrates skills or aptitudes useful in libraries," said Ginger Williams (Wichita State University).

Setting up a social media page for a club? Designing a spreadsheet/database to track entries for a local walk-a-thon? Writing press releases for local author visits to bookstores? Setting up booths for a regional comic convention? We love library experience, but if you have non-library experience in communicating, marketing, or organizing information, think about how it would translate into a library setting.

Use Your Network

Spread the word that you're looking for a job. If you don't need to keep your search a secret from your current employer, then tell everyone you know that you are job hunting. Email your entire contact list, post your search on social networking sites, ask your friends to tell their friends. Use every networking contact you have. These contacts can tell you about job openings, suggest places to look, and keep their ears open for possibilities to share with you. Let people know what you can do, especially if you have skills beyond traditional library work, so that they can connect the dots between your skills and potential job opportunities.

One caveat about sharing your job search status on social networking sites: keep it professional. Don't complain about your current job, your boss, or your latest interview. Don't share too much information about your interactions with potential employers—for example, "I rocked that interview at X Library!" or "That loser Z Corporation has never even contacted me about my application!" As we discussed in chapter 4, be discreet and professional when emailing or posting information online. Assume that potential employers may read what you write.

What if you do need to keep your job search a secret from your current employer? Well, first, ask a trusted friend: do you really need to keep it a secret? Most employers recognize that an employee who is finishing a graduate degree will be looking for a new job. You will probably find that your boss fully expects you to leave after graduation and would be disappointed if you didn't pursue other jobs. If you truly do need to keep your search a secret, then share your search only with trusted friends. Ask others such as trusted coworkers, customers, clients, or faculty members to serve as job references on your resume.

CONCLUSION

Take time to assess yourself before you begin your search. Your goals and interests will change over time, so reassess yourself periodically throughout your career. Organize your time and materials to search more efficiently. Broaden your search options as much as possible to improve your chances of finding a job more quickly.

WORKS CITED

Dority, G. Kim. *Rethinking Information Work: A Career Guide for Librarians and Other Information Professionals*. Westport, CT: Libraries Unlimited, 2006.

Gordon, Rachel Singer. *What's the Alternative?: Career Options for Librarians and Info Pros*. Medford, NJ: Information Today, 2008.

Shontz, Priscilla K., and Richard A. Murray, editors. *A Day in the Life: Career Options in Library and Information Science*. Westport, CT: Libraries Unlimited, 2007.

CHAPTER 8

Resumes

Forget this. You can't learn anything from a resume. So, tell me about your employment history.

Malcolm in the Middle, 2003

Writing a resume can seem like a daunting task. How do you effectively sell yourself on paper to a potential employer? How can you create a resume that makes an employer want to know more about you?

COMPILE YOUR WORK HISTORY

Before you begin writing, first write down everything you've done. While all of this information will not make its way onto your resume, it's essential to compile a comprehensive master list that you can use later. You will use various bits of information from this document when you create various resumes and cover letters. You'll often need this information when filling out applications.

List your work history, including both your paid jobs and any unpaid work such as volunteer work and internships. Write down your start and end dates (month and year) for these jobs. Under each position, jot down any accomplishments you can think of. Try to think of specific, quantifiable accomplishments if possible. For example, did you supervise a certain number of student employees or typically catalog a certain number of items per week? Also write down your job duties in each position. Note your supervisor's name and contact information, and your starting and ending salary, because some job applications ask for this information.

As you accumulate more experience, you'll forget a lot of the dates and tasks from your earlier positions, so hold on to this list. You'll be surprised at how hard it is to remember these details ten years from now! Update the list periodically, even when you are not searching for a job, to make future job hunts easier.

Write down all degrees earned and schools attended, along with locations, start dates, and end dates. Note your major and minor areas of study. List any clubs, organizations, awards, research projects, and other information about your educational experiences. You may also want to list the courses you took in library school or keep a copy of your transcript.

Write down any publications, presentations, awards and honors, professional memberships, or activities that you have participated in. Include dates when relevant—for example, what years were you president of your student group, or when did you win that award? List any language or technical skills.

Collect supporting materials. Create a file or portfolio of your work. You may want to include documents like research papers, handouts you created for your job, thank you letters from clients, and so on. Include copies of any publications. Even if you don't show these documents to prospective employers, they give you a record of your own accomplishments. You may look back at these documents with surprise someday when you have forgotten all about them! You can sometimes build on these projects or ideas to develop future projects, publications, or presentations.

CONSIDER YOUR TRANSFERABLE SKILLS

One of your greatest challenges may be showing a potential employer how your skills are useful in a different environment. Think about how you can make those skills more visible; you can also do some of this in a cover letter and interview. Don't make the people who are reading your resume try to guess how your disparate experiences have given you skills that are applicable to the job they're trying to fill; make those connections for them. When looking at a job ad, go down the list of required and preferred qualifications and write down what experience you have that directly relates to each item. Then try to emphasize those qualifications in your resume, cover letter, and interview.

"The biggest problem that I see with students' resumes and cover letters is that they consistently undersell themselves, failing to mention critical skills and job experience, or understating their actual abilities, skills, and knowledge," advised Karen Cook (Clarion University).

This also comes into play when they need to distinguish themselves from the professional librarians they are competing against for job positions. They have probably been immersed in some of the latest theoretical discussions, exposed to the most current thinking regarding best practices, and learned about and/or used the very latest in software and technology. Because the students have a reasonable concern about their lack of experience compared with others already in the job market, they don't think to stress the advantages of their own up-to-date knowledge and skills. Also, many students disregard the actual experience many have had either working in libraries or in non-library settings, both paid and unpaid.

TAILOR EACH RESUME

After collecting all your data, you're ready to begin writing your resume or resumes. Every time you apply for a job, tailor your resume to that specific job ad. Don't just send the same resume out to every position you apply for. Your cover letter and resume should directly respond to each specific point listed in each job ad. Employers emphasized that one size does not fit all. "Not addressing why they want *this* job at *this* university is a huge no-no," said Chris Nolan.

That's where the big master list of information comes in handy. You can pull data from that list to put together a resume that shows how you meet the job requirements.

Begin by creating a few basic resumes. Let's say that your top job choice would be a public services position in an academic library, but you'd also be interested in working in a special library or public library. Choose a few job ads that interest you, ones that sound most like a job you would like, and build a resume for each type of position. Building a few types of "base" resumes gives you a starting point so that you can adapt your resume for each job ad that interests you. For example, you might create three basic resume files called Academic, Special, and Public. When you see a specific public library job opening that you'd like to apply for, start with your basic public library resume and adapt it to match the job ad.

CHOOSE A RESUME FORMAT

Resumes typically fall into three formats: chronological, functional, and a combination of the two styles. The most commonly used format, the chronological format, lists your work history and education in reverse date order with the most recent at the top. Most employers prefer this type because it's familiar and easy to read quickly. It emphasizes your job progression. However, it can also emphasize gaps in employment or a history of short-term employment.

The functional format organizes your work experience into major skill groups. This may work well for career changers, especially if you wish to downplay your current job. This format allows you to emphasize transferable skills and to combine skills gained in unrelated fields. Some candidates with large employment gaps prefer to use a functional format. However, many employers are suspicious of this format because it may appear that you are trying to hide something. They often find this format more difficult to read and feel it makes them work harder to find the information they want. In his article "Gaps in Your Resume," John Lehner wrote:

> Unless you really do have something to hide, be wary of using this approach. I have frequently seen search committees respond negatively to this approach. Hiring officials and search committees may tend to make negative inferences if they suspect a candidate is trying to hide something.

The combination format combines the chronological and functional formats. List your work experience and education in reverse date order, but under those job title headings, group types of experience under skill headings that match the job listing. This format allows you to emphasize relevant skills while maintaining the chronological history. This format is more difficult to design in a visually appealing and concise presentation, but it can be useful for showing how your diverse experience relates to the desired job.

BUILDING YOUR RESUME: COMMON COMPONENTS

We highly recommend Robert Newlen's book *Resume Writing and Interviewing Techniques That Work!* for step-by-step advice and sample resumes. This chapter will highlight some of the most common recommendations we've received from employers about what they like and dislike in a resume.

Contact Information

Give your name at the top of your resume. You may want to use a larger font size than you use elsewhere in the document. Include your name on every page in case pages get separated.

List your address, phone numbers, and email address. It is best to use a home address and personal phone number and email account. Use a personal email address that sounds professional. Don't use a cute email name like "2hot4u@gmail.com." Don't use the email account from your current job. You should also consider what your phone's voice mail message might sound like to a prospective employer who calls you.

If you have an online portfolio, list it with your contact information. If you have a professional Web site, you could list it here, but you may want to list it elsewhere in your resume.

Job Objectives and Qualifications

While some experts recommend including a job objective and statement of qualifications, we don't recommend these. Many employers feel that these waste space that is at a premium in a resume. As Susanne Markgren (Purchase College, SUNY) said, "It's obvious what their objective is: to get the job." Instead of summarizing your top qualifications at the beginning of your resume, highlight them in your cover letter, and use your resume to expand on those qualifications. John Lehner agreed, "I don't find the objective to be at all valuable. The cover letter should be used to explain your interest in the specific position you are seeking."

However, some experts and employers feel that these sections are helpful. In his resume book, Robert Newlen encouraged applicants to include these statements and provided examples for formatting them. Kim Dority said that these points "may help organize and present what the applicant feels is valuable and distinctive." Lorene Flanders commented that she "has seen this rarely and would find it helpful when there are dozens of applicants."

Education

If you are a current student with very little work experience, you may want to list your education before your experience. If you have a great deal of library experience, definitely list your experience first. Employers are more interested in relevant experience than coursework. Under the heading, list education information in reverse chronological order.

- Degree awarded
- School and location
- Year of degree
- Major and minor (optional)
- Honors (cum laude, etc.)

You don't have to spell out commonly understood acronyms such as BA or MS. For a library audience, you can list MLS or MLIS. For a non-library reader, spell out these degrees. Educational work that didn't lead to a degree, or is still in progress, should be listed in the same format as your degrees. For example:

Education

M.A. Psychology, Montana State University, Bozeman, MT, 2012–present
M.S. Library Science, University of North Texas, Denton, TX, 2012
B.A. Communication, University of Texas at Arlington, 2008
    Major in journalism; minor in psychology

It's typically not helpful to list individual courses that you took. Most library employers know what type of courses students take in a library science program. If you feel that you have taken specialized courses that directly relate to the job, you may want to list them, but practical experience, special projects, and publications always carry more weight than coursework.

You may list continuing education in the education section or in a separate section, typically near the end of the resume. Some applicants list continuing education under Professional Development. Continuing education can show an employer that you are committed to learning more or staying current in a certain subject area.

Work Experience

This is the most important section of your resume and the one that will take up the most space. Using your master list of accomplishments or the basic resumes you created earlier, tailor each resume to each job ad by highlighting the experience and skills that relate directly to that job. Because search committees usually work with a checklist of qualifications, you want to make it easy for them to see how you match their requirements. When revising your resume to match a job ad, you might reword a bullet point or move a bullet point higher under a certain job title to emphasize that accomplishment. Reread your resume carefully to see how it matches the qualifications for the job.

Sometimes it's effective to list volunteer experience along with your paid work experience under the Work Experience heading. Emphasizing relevant volunteer experience is especially helpful for new graduates, career changers, and people with employment gaps. Don't be afraid to emphasize the skills you've gained through volunteer work, especially if that volunteer position relates more directly to the desired job than your paid job does. Highlight the skills that the employer wants, whether they were gained through paid or unpaid experience.

Work Experience Subheadings

List your experience in reverse date order. List the job titles in bold font. Include the job title, organization, location, and dates of employment. If the organization name makes the location obvious, it's not necessary to list it, but consistent headings are more visually appealing. To be consistent, include the same type of information in the same order in each subheading. Make sure the job titles are easy for the reader to spot, as employers generally care more about *what* you did than *where* you did it. For example:

Circulation Supervisor, Galbraith Library, Chicago, IL   2006–2009

Or you could list the organization on a separate line, like this:

Circulation Supervisor   2006–2009
Galbraith Library, Chicago, IL

If you have held several jobs within the same organization, you may wish to list the organization first and then list each job as a separate subheading under that organization's name. This format emphasizes your longevity at one workplace, but it deemphasizes your job titles. For example:

Richards Nature Resource Center, San Diego, CA

- Environmental Education Program Specialist, 2008–present
- Administrative Assistant, 2004–2008

Listing months of employment is unnecessary unless you held a short-term position. For example:

Intern, Boeker International Library, Atlanta, GA   Jan–May 2010

Work Experience Bulleted Lists

Under each job heading, list a few accomplishments or responsibilities. Make sure you don't sound like you are copying your job description. Employers already know what you were supposed to do on the job. What did you actually *do?* Creating these bulleted lists is one of the most critical sections of a resume. There are some basic steps to keep in mind as you compose this part of your resume.

Use Active Verbs

Begin each list item with an action verb. These verbs make you sound like someone who gets things done. Listing concrete accomplishments makes you come alive to the reader. Try to be active, descriptive, specific, and quantifiable. For example, instead of "planning, promoting and executing literacy activities," which is pretty vague, try to think of something more active and specific, such as "taught students to use library databases" or "read to 800+ students weekly during class story times." Give the reader a vivid mental image of who you are and what you did.

Quantify and Specify Your Achievements

Quantify your accomplishments as much as you can. For example, instead of saying "responsible for reference services," say "served 20 hours per week at the general reference desk" or "provided reference assistance to more than 2000 students at the art library reference desk."

Use this tactic to demonstrate productivity; for example, "reformatted summer camp programs resulting in a 60% increase in attendance" sounds more vibrant than "managed summer camp programs." Statements like "taught 15 library instruction sessions per semester" and "cataloged a collection of 1600 Colombian gift books" tell potential employers much more about what you did than "performed library instruction" or "processed gift books."

You should also be specific about your activities; say what you mean. Try to avoid vague words like "helped" or "participated." Instead of "helped with library exhibits," tell what you did and how many exhibits you worked on.

Be Clear

Use direct, plain language instead of "academic-speak" or jargon, and avoid acronyms unless you are sure the reader will immediately understand them. A hiring supervisor at a library will probably know what "WorldCat" is, but a hiring supervisor at a law firm might not; in that case, a phrase like "the WorldCat international bibliographic database" might be more appropriate.

Be Consistent

Make sure all tenses are consistent. Don't flip back and forth between past and present tense. Use verbs or verb phrases consistently throughout your resume, and don't alternate between nouns, adjectives, and verbs. For example, avoid using inconsistent headings such as these:

- Responsible for cataloging special collections materials
- Supervised 3 student employees

Instead, use a verb for every bullet point, like this:

- Cataloged special collections materials
- Supervised 3 student employees

Limit Yourself

Most resume experts recommend limiting your bullet points under each job to about three or four items. Often you will find that you may need more than four points under your current job, or whichever job is most relevant to the position you're applying for. But most other jobs, especially the ones in your more distant past, should have just a few under them. As time goes by those early jobs may become just a job title with no bullet points under them, or they may disappear altogether. Seeing too many bullet points under your job titles overwhelms the reader. You don't want the reader to toss your resume in the "no" pile at first glance! List the top three or four accomplishments for each job you've had. Of course, your bullet points may change on each resume you create because you want to match the wording and qualifications listed in that specific job ad.

Some academic library search committees prefer a very thorough resume that lists great detail about each position. In these cases, feel free to list more bullet points, but don't pad the list with things that are obvious. For example, if you worked in a circulation department, you probably shelved books, but you don't need to waste space mentioning that. Make sure that what you list really relates to the skills and requirements listed in that particular job ad. Seeing 12 bullet points for one job title is visually overwhelming, and an employer may assume you're padding your resume. Don't eliminate relevant points, but streamline in order to emphasize relevant qualifications. Reread your bullet points, thinking about how each point relates to the job ad. This is why your master accomplishment list is so handy; you may use different items in each resume.

Volunteer Work

If your volunteer experience is current, list it with your paid experience to emphasize relevant library skills. However, if your experience is not current or is in an unrelated field, you may choose to list that work in a separate Volunteer Experience section. You might include this section immediately after your Experience section, or if it's less relevant, you might list it after other additional sections.

Structure a Volunteer Experience section just as you did the Experience section. Here's your chance to mention skills or experience you've gained in unpaid positions. For example, perhaps you supervised other volunteers, managed a budget, raised money, wrote for publications, or planned programs. Highlight skills that may not show up in your Experience section. Don't discount community or non-library-related volunteer work. You may have gained some extremely useful transferable skills through volunteer positions.

This is an example of how you might list volunteer experience on a resume:

Story Time Volunteer, Children's Center, Emporia, KS 2008–2010
- Planned weekly story time and read books to children (ages 3–5)
- Led craft activities

Additional Information

As we discussed in chapter 5, extracurricular activities help you stand out in any applicant pool, especially one for an entry-level position. Academic libraries in particular expect librarians to perform in three areas: librarianship (your job duties), service (being involved in professional associations), and research (writing and publishing). They'll be looking for those accomplishments in your resume.

Presentations and Publications

If you have presented or published, be sure to list these items, even if they are not library related. If you have several publications and presentations, use two separate sections, one for publications and one for presentations. If you have only a few items to list, combine these in one Publications and Presentations section.

For presentations, give the title, where and when you gave it, and name any copresenters you may have had. Include poster sessions, brown bag sessions, teaching experience, and any other experience that demonstrates your public speaking skills. For example:

> "Metadata for Photograph Collections." Ontario Library Association Annual Conference, Ottawa, Ontario, April 2010
> "Study Abroad Programs for Library Science Students." Presented with Lisa Smith to Student Chapter of ALA, University of North Carolina at Chapel Hill School of Information & Library Science, December 2011

Here's how you might list non-library teaching experience:

> Champaign County Forest Preserve District, 2003–2008
> Eco-Adventures Day Camp Program (ages 3–12)
> Environmental Education Programs (ages 6–18)

For your publications, use a standard form of citation, such as APA or *Chicago Manual of Style*. It doesn't matter which one you pick; the important thing is that you pick one and use it consistently in your Publications section. Include any publications, including blogs or online articles, that demonstrate to the employer that you know how to write and are familiar with the publication process.

Professional Involvement

Create a section on your resume with a name such as Professional Involvement or Service. In this section, list organizations you've joined and participated in at the local, regional, or national level. You might wish to include non-library groups; your participation may demonstrate your organizational skills, productivity, or ability to be an active member of a team. Be cautious about listing religious or political groups, as you risk turning a potential employer off. When combining library and non-library involvement into one section, you may want to use a general heading such as Service, possibly listing your service under subheadings such as Library Service and Community Service. For example:

Service

Library

Member, North American Serials Interest Group Continuing Education Committee, 2007–2009

Community

Volunteer Coordinator, Northampton Elementary Parent-Faculty Organization, 2011–2012

If you've served as a committee member or chair, emphasize your leadership roles. You could create separate sections for Service (active participation) and Memberships (organizations that you've joined). For example:

Professional Involvement

Committees and Leadership

American Library Association New Members Round Table

Student Chapter of the Year Award Committee, 2009 to Present

Memberships

Special Libraries Association, 2008 to Present

ALA Library Instruction Round Table, 2008 to Present

Alternatively, you could combine your activities into one Professional Involvement section, noting your level of participation in each organization just as you would a job title. For example:

Professional Involvement

Chair, ALA New Members Round Table President's Program Committee, 2010–2011

Member, New Mexico Library Association, 2007–present

Technical Skills

Many resumes include a Technology Skills section. In this section you might list your knowledge of or experience with Web design, databases, office software, or other relevant experience, especially if the job requires familiarity with those tools. For example, employers often prefer a candidate who is already familiar with the databases they use. The job ad may list some resources by name, but if not, look at the library's Web site to see what they use. Try to show in your resume or cover letter that you already know how to use the databases and tools that they value.

Language Skills

If you are proficient in one or more foreign languages, include a Language Skills section. If appropriate, distinguish between different levels of language proficiency: native fluency, conversational, reading knowledge, bibliographic knowledge, and the like. It's essential to include this information if the job specifically calls for knowledge of a particular language, but include it even if the vacancy announcement doesn't ask for language skills.

Awards and Honors

If you have won awards, earned honors, or been recognized in some other way, include a section to mention that information. This isn't the place to share that you were your high school's homecoming queen or that you won your local chili cook-off competition, but list library-related, academic, or community recognition that enhances your professional image.

Hobbies, Interests, or Personal Information

Don't list personal information such as hobbies, interests, pets, marital status, children, religious affiliation, favorite colors, or sign of the zodiac. A resume shouldn't resemble a dating Web site profile! Including personal information makes you appear less professional and increases the risk of alienating the reader.

Job References

It's common for employers to require a few job references. Line up some people who will speak positively about you and your work performance. These might include current or former supervisors, coworkers, or teachers. If you've worked on a professional association committee or collaborated on a project or presentation, you might list people you worked with. The people you list could vary depending on the job you're applying for.

What if you would prefer not to list your current employer? Perhaps you aren't ready to broadcast your job search or you're not sure your supervisor will give you a glowing review. In this case, list a coworker who can speak about your performance in your current job. Perhaps you could list others you've worked with in your current job: a supervisor in a different department, a faculty member, or a library customer you've helped. If you are a finalist, the employer will want to talk with your supervisor, so at that stage you will have to tell that you are interviewing.

Ask permission before you list someone as a reference. Give your references a copy of your latest resume, or a list of your accomplishments, to refresh their memories about your activities. Alert them if you think an employer may contact them. Don't let them be surprised by a phone call from an employer.

"References are critical to your being offered the job," said April Pavis.

Discuss with your references (before you put them on the list) that you would like to use them, and what projects, assignments, duties, or abilities you want them to highlight. Being a reference for someone else is very humbling and also important. What they say can sway the interviewer between you and another applicant. If you get the job, send a thank you to each of your references letting them know that they will no longer receive any phone calls because you landed the job. Thank them profusely; then stay in contact with them, because you may need each other in the future.

GENERAL GUIDELINES

Length

Students and recent graduates ask how long their resumes should be. A number of arbitrary rules are floating around about how long is too long. The fictional but widely circulated myth is that a resume should never, ever be more than one page long. A good rule of thumb is to use as much space as it takes. As a student or recent graduate, unless you have extensive library experience or a voluminous list of publications, your resume will probably fit on two pages. Don't pad to try to make yourself look more accomplished or world-renowned than you actually are; employers will see through that. If you're changing careers, your challenge may be determining which key transferable skills to showcase in your resume. Pare down your non-library experience to highlight your abilities without overwhelming the employer with extraneous details.

In general, resumes are typically longer and more detailed for academic library jobs than for positions in public or special libraries. Resumes should be even shorter for non-library jobs. Steve Oberg said:

I was used to presenting an exhaustive resume for academic jobs. I think a more thoughtful, pared-down resume that is organized and presented in an entirely different way has more of an impact in the for-profit environment. For instance, focus on presenting your skills and relevant experience first and foremost. Summarize and synthesize your experience more. Be absolutely sure that you have the credentials for the job in hand and that these are easily identified in your resume. No one has a lot of time to review resumes and taking this extra effort really makes the review process easier.

Mechanics and Style

Use plain white paper and plain black ink. Using neon yellow paper or typing your headings in red lettering won't get your resume noticed in a good way. Most resumes will be photocopied many times, so patterns or colors won't copy well, and extremely thick, heavy paper may jam the copier. It sounds minor, but you don't want to annoy your potential employers by causing unnecessary problems.

Use a clean, professional, easy-to-read font. Bold each heading to make them easier to pick out. Include enough white space in the margins and between headings or sections to make the resume visually attractive and uncluttered. Your goal is to draw the reader in and make it extremely easy for that person to notice your qualifications.

Include your name at the top of every page; sometimes pages get separated when an employer makes multiple copies for search committee members. You can use your word processing software's header function to do this; for example, "Smith, p. 2."

Language, Spelling, and Grammar

Spell check! Be sure to spell all names accurately. Double check all the spelling. "Poor grammar, misspellings, and other evidence of lack of attention to detail often prejudice me against a candidate before ever taking a hard look at their actual experience," said Clint Chamberlain. Don't depend on your word processor's spell check to catch all the errors. Ask a friend, coworker, or someone else you trust to look over your resume before you send it to catch anything you may have missed.

Be consistent throughout the document. Remove periods from the end of headings. If you put periods at the end of bulleted list items, be sure to put periods at the end of every one. Keep everything consistent throughout your resume: fonts, heading styles, dates, spacing, tenses, and so on. If you use past tense, use it all the way through.

Use language that is as specific, active, and quantifiable as possible. Avoid jargon and acronyms unless they are instantly understandable. Use plain, direct language. Make sure you address the requirements being asked for in the job posting, but avoid sounding like you are simply regurgitating a job description.

When applying to a non-library job, describe your work as if you were talking to someone who knows nothing about library internal workings.

Get a friend or relative who doesn't know library jargon to read your resume and see whether it makes sense.

DIGITAL RESUMES

Some jobs ask for a digital version of your resume. Create a plain text version of your resume or, even better, a PDF (unless the employer has specifically asked for some other file type). A PDF works well because you keep control over the formatting and the way it will look on the recipient's screen. Wendy Israel said, "About ninety percent of my applications were electronic, so I turned my cover letter and resume into one PDF file for each application."

Many organizations use electronic search tools to narrow down the applicant pool. To help your resume rise to the top of the pile, embed relevant keywords throughout your resume. Use key terms from the job ad in your resume. Because computers sometimes count the number of times keywords are used, try to repeat the most important words (in an appropriate way, of course) throughout your resume to increase the odds that the computer will find more matches.

Nellie Moffitt (Navy Installations Command) described the federal government screening process.

If you do not explain what it is you do, HR makes no assumptions; you'll not get past the automated systems that determine if your resume makes the cut. HR determines if you make the cut, not the selecting official. The candidates that are sent to the selecting official may not reflect the best of the bunch, but they are the best at using the correct terms to make it past HR and the automated systems.

ONLINE PORTFOLIOS

by Susanne Markgren (co-author, Career Q&A with the Library Career People)

An online portfolio can be a strategic tool for today's job-seeking librarian. It allows potential employers to explore your professional and educational materials and your work experience in greater depth than they can by reading your resume and cover letter. Because of this, an online portfolio may give you an advantage over other candidates.

What Is an Online Portfolio?

In its most basic form, an online portfolio is your resume deconstructed on a Web site. It can serve as a storage space for important professional documents, as a professional and creative display space, or as a simple way to share and archive your professional materials.

How to Create an Online Portfolio

You can create an online portfolio using a free, hosted tool that you might use to create a wiki, blog, or Web site. Choose something that allows you to upload a variety of different document types, provides you with enough storage space for your materials, does not contain ads, allows you to customize with your own designs, and offers a way to limit access should you choose to not have it open to everyone. These tools usually come with built-in functionality like a search box, tagging, comments, pages, and a rich text editor, which makes it easy for someone with limited technical skills to create a professional-looking online portfolio.

What to Include in Your Online Portfolio

Start by copying and pasting everything that is in your resume, and then add more detail. If you are a student or recent graduate, include information about classes you took, projects you worked on, and library-related work experience such as jobs, internships, volunteer work, and so on. If you wrote a thesis or a research paper, include that in your portfolio. If you don't have experience working in libraries, include other experience that highlights transferable skills. You can also add a personal statement, research interests, design work, writing samples, awards and grants, and an RSS feed to your Twitter account or blog.

Tips for Designing Your Portfolio

- Create different pages, categories, or tabs to improve navigation and design.
- Upload or embed items and documents that you own; link to ones you do not.
- Include materials that you would show your current employer.
- Make it easy for people to contact you: include your name and email address. You may also want to include links to your professional social networks.
- Use tags/keywords (if available) to help in searching.
- Be creative. Your portfolio shouldn't be just an online replica of your resume.
- Upload a printable PDF version of your resume.

- Keep it current.
- Use it to promote yourself. Your online portfolio is a link; use it in your email signature, link to it from your resume, and include it in your cover letters and social media profiles.

How to Market Your Online Portfolio

Once you've created your online portfolio, you want it to be seen. The best way to do this is to create professional profiles on popular sites like LinkedIn, Academia.edu, or ALA Connect and link to your portfolio from these sites. If you're already using social media tools such as Facebook and Twitter, you can link to your portfolio from the profile pages of those sites. You should also create a Google profile, which will display in the first page of Google results when your name is searched. By creating professional profiles and using your online portfolio to promote your professional identity, you push the "good stuff" to the top of the pile; when people search for you online, they will find what you want them to find.

CONCLUSION

Your resume is your opportunity to show employers what you have to offer. A great resume will help your application float to the top, while a bad one can immediately land in the "no thanks" pile.

Use your resume to summarize your key qualifications for the job you're applying for. Present your information in a clear, concise, consistent way; if employers have to work too hard to figure out whether you meet their needs, they'll lose interest and move on to another resume. By keeping in mind what employers want to see, you can design a resume that makes a positive impression and prompts employers to want to find out more about you.

WORKS CITED

Lehner, John. "Gaps in Your Resume: Addressing an Interruption in Your Career Path," http://liscareer.com/lehner_gap.htm (cited October 11, 2011).

Newlen, Robert. *Resume Writing and Interviewing Techniques That Work!: A How-to-Do-It Manual for Librarians.* New York: Neal-Schuman, 2006.

CHAPTER 9

Cover Letters

Well, the first thing you should have is an idea and then . . . Well, first you need something to write with . . . Well, obviously you need a writing instrument and you need an idea. I'm just not sure which should come first.

Bones, 2006

A common mistake many job seekers make is to spend a lot of time creating a strong resume and then treat the cover letter as an afterthought. When you're applying for a job, first impressions are paramount, and your cover letter is often the first piece of information a potential employer receives about you. One of the fastest ways to land your application in the "no" pile is to send a cover letter that's generic, sloppy, or alienating. "Cover letters are given tons of weight at my institution," said Samantha Schmehl Hines. "If the letter is not good, we often don't even look at the resume." This chapter is designed to help you avoid some common pitfalls and write a cover letter that makes a reader want to know more about you.

WHAT'S THE PURPOSE OF A COVER LETTER?

Many misconceptions exist about what a cover letter is or what it's supposed to accomplish. Some people think a cover letter is just a form letter in which you introduce yourself and explain what a great person you are. Others believe a cover letter should rephrase the information that's found in a resume to present it in a flowery prose form instead of in a bulleted list. Still others feel a cover letter should just be a paragraph saying, "Please find attached my resume and here are my name and address so you will know where to send the job offer." None of these notions are correct.

The cover letter serves a very specific purpose: it is a bridge between you and the job you are applying for. The cover letter should explain why your work experience, education, and skills make you the best candidate for the *specific job* you're applying for. What does this mean? It means you read through the vacancy announcement and address point by point how you can do the things they're asking for.

You should start from scratch with each letter and tailor it to the job you're applying for at that moment. This is sometimes the hardest thing for people to understand, but it's absolutely crucial. Job applicants often make the mistake of having a stock cover letter saved somewhere. They open the file, change the date and the name of the library, print out a new copy, and shove it into an envelope. This is the worst way you can approach a cover letter. Directors, search committees, and HR departments don't want to feel like they're reading a generic cover letter. Nancy Agafetei said, "A generic letter not applicable to my job opening is an immediate turn-off."

You may be applying for lots of jobs, but Library X doesn't care about that. The people at Library X only care about Library X, and specifically about this vacancy they're trying to fill. Therefore, they want to see that you've given this job a lot of thought and can convince them that you're the best person for it. Don't just tell them you are a great person in general. That may well be, but that's not what Library X cares about right now. Your cover letter must say "Here's why I'm right for this job," not just "Here's who I am and what I know." Kim Dority cautioned that a letter that "focuses on an applicant's needs and interests rather than on how she or he could bring value to the organization" is likely to turn off potential employers.

How does this work in practice? The first thing you need to do, before you even open up a blank document and start writing, is to read the job description. Then read it several more times. Think about how your background has prepared you to do this job, and how you are going to convey that to your potential employers. What tasks have you performed in your jobs, field experiences, or internships that are similar to what the library is asking this person to do? What courses have you taken in library school that are related to this job, and, more specifically, what did you do in those courses that is relevant? For example, if you're applying for a job with collection development responsibilities, don't just tell them you took the required collection development class in school; tell them about a specific project you worked on in that class, or research you did, or a paper you wrote.

What other things have you done that relate to this job? Think about workshops or conferences you've attended, training you've had, or anything else that's relevant. You may have to be creative. This means thinking critically about your background and the skills and knowledge you've gained, even in other types of jobs or environments. If you're applying for a job as a children's librarian, by all means tell them that you used to be an elementary school teacher or that you worked in a daycare. If this job involves supervisory responsibilities, tell them about the retail job you had where you managed staff. Don't make ridiculously tenuous connections or stretch the truth, however. It might take more than creativity to convince them that the summer you spent pumping frozen yogurt prepared you to repair and preserve ancient manuscripts.

Your cover letter should have a logical flow of information through it. Don't make confusing leaps like telling how much you love nineteenth-century Russian literature and that is why you are interested in their job as a Spanish-language cataloger, or that your experience as a middle school librarian has prepared you to be a photo archivist. While there may very well be links between what seem like disparate areas of your interests or background, it's your job to delineate those connections. Don't give potential employers whiplash by suddenly changing directions without explaining how you got there.

Some things they're asking for in the job vacancy ad may be ones that you don't have experience in or knowledge of. That's okay. It does mean, however, that you will really have to sell the areas in which you do.

Keep the vacancy announcement in front of you as you're writing your cover letter. You may find it helpful to print out a copy of it and check off the important parts as you address them. It's sometimes a good idea to repeat back some of the same language the institution has used in the job posting, especially if there are particular phrases that they use multiple times. Don't go overboard with this, though. As with your resume, you don't want them to feel you're just parroting back what they said in the vacancy announcement.

What might this look like? If one of the job duties included in the posting is "Provides reference services at a busy public library branch," you could say something like, "Spending six months as a reference intern at Rifkin College Library taught me how to get to the heart of reference questions, which databases are most useful to patrons, and how to provide quality service at a busy desk," and follow it up with another sentence or two about your background or interest in reference work. Even though your experience is not in a public library, you mention the similar experience you *do* have, and then give some details that address what they're probably looking for. The fact that they call themselves "a busy public library branch" means their reference librarians probably deal with a lot of people passing through, the phone ringing, and emails coming in. This is your cue to volunteer information about how you learned to provide quality service in your own hectic environment while working the desk during finals week, answering the phone while also keeping an eye on reference questions coming in via instant message, or answering questions at the reference desk and also helping patrons troubleshoot technical difficulties in the adjacent information commons.

Here's another example: the vacancy announcement mentions that one of the job responsibilities is cataloging books in Spanish. You don't have that exact experience, but you have a combination of complementary experiences. You did a semester-long internship in the order management section of your college library, where you searched OCLC for bibliographic records for AV materials, brought those records into the local catalog, and attached order records to them. You also took a cataloging class in library school, and you studied Spanish for two years as an undergrad. You have all the cards to make a solid poker hand; you just have to lay them out on the table for your potential employer to see. Of course, this won't work if one of the *required* qualifications is at least five years doing original cataloging of Spanish books. But if Spanish cataloging experience is merely *preferred*, or just mentioned as one of several duties this person will be performing, you can use your cover letter to connect the dots and explain how your background has prepared you to do the job even if it's not immediately apparent on your resume.

Besides tailoring your letter to the job, you should tailor your letter to the institution. This means you should do a little research on the library and incorporate it as appropriate into your cover letter. Look at their Web site and see what kinds of interesting initiatives they are involved in or projects they are working on. For example, if their Web site mentions that they're doing a big building renovation, you could mention how you envision this position being involved in providing services in the new physical environment. Search committee members like to feel that you have put some effort into this application and that you've taken the time to learn something about their library. Don't throw in insincere flattery ("Your Web site is the greatest thing I have ever seen!"); approach your statements thoughtfully. Show them that you're truly interested in what they're doing and want to be part of their team.

BEGINNINGS AND ENDINGS

The body of your cover letter is where the real substance is, but there are also a few things to keep in mind with the opening and closing. Include your contact information, including mail and email addresses and a phone number, at the top of the page. Although you've included this on your resume, remember that your cover letter and resume may get separated at some point during the screening process.

The vacancy announcement may have the name of a contact person to whom you should send your application. If so, name that person in your salutation: "Dear Ms. Blackmon." If no name is included, you can go to the library's Web site, find the name of its director, and address your cover letter to that person. It's also appropriate to begin with something like "Dear members of the search committee." Avoid "To whom it may concern" because it can appear cold and too generic.

Include the name of the position and where you saw it advertised. In the first paragraph, your potential employer should know what you're applying for and how you found out about it. Libraries often have multiple vacancies at the same time and are therefore running several searches simultaneously. They don't want to have to guess which of their jobs you're applying for. "Don't send a cover letter or email that doesn't state which job you are applying for," said Diane Calvin. "When two or three searches are underway, the dean's office has to contact the applicant for clarification. This makes the applicant look less detail-oriented."

At the same time, you should tell them where you saw the vacancy posted. This tells them where their advertising is being seen, and it also demonstrates that you know how to look at a Web site, subscribe to an electronic mailing list, read a newspaper ad, or interact with the outside world in some way. For example, "I am applying for the position of Youth Services Librarian, which I saw on ALA JobList." If a position number is included in the vacancy announcement, include that, too.

Your cover letter should close with a positive statement regarding future action. For example, "I look forward to speaking with you." You don't need to repeat your contact information in this sentence (as in "Please contact me at 867-5309") because you have listed it at the top of your letter.

STYLE MATTERS

Now that we've talked about the philosophy of a cover letter and the content you should include, how do you convey all that appropriately? You're introducing yourself to people you want to work for, so approach your letter as you would an in-person interview. As with your resume, your cover letter is professional correspondence, so don't be too casual; strive for an engaging tone that is direct and concise. Don't try to be too formal or write in the style we call "academic-ese." Now is not the time to trot out your GRE vocabulary words or write long, convoluted sentences with lots of semicolons and dependent clauses. Read your letter out loud, and if it doesn't sound natural, or like something an actual human being would ever say, revise it. Be professional without being pretentious. If you are quoting Voltaire or Plato, you're probably off track.

You should also be positive. This isn't the place to say bad things about your current or previous employers. Remember that your cover letter is the first time these people are "meeting" you, and if you start out by immediately badmouthing other people you've worked with, you'll come across as a malcontent and will also make them wonder what you'll say about them behind their backs if you get the job. Your cover letter should be about why you want to work for Library X, not why you are trying to get away from your current job at Library Y. Treat this as business correspondence; be conservative in formatting and presentation. A cover letter is not the place to be whimsical or fun. Stick with a classic font like Times New Roman, not something cute like Comic Sans Serif; it's a good idea to use the same font and style you used on your resume so the two documents complement each other. If you are sending in a printed copy instead of submitting your materials electronically, use a good quality printer and nice white paper.

Don't be gimmicky. You might be amazed at the things some job applicants include in cover letters in the hope of getting the potential employer's attention. Remember, there *is* such a thing as bad attention. As Chris Nolan said, "Self-confidence is good, but the overly assertive 'I'm exactly who you need, you can stop your search now!' letters are over the top and downgrade my view of that candidate." There should be no exclamation points in your letter. You're writing a cover letter, not posting on your friend's Facebook wall. If you find that you're beginning to sound like someone shouting about magical cleaning products on a TV commercial, stop what you're doing, take a deep breath, and start over.

Don't include extraneous information, especially of a personal nature. This is a cover letter, not a personals ad. It's very nice that you own more than 300 model trains or that you grow barley in your backyard or that you are in the *Guinness Book of World Records* for something you ate, but your cover letter is not the place to explain all this *unless* it is related to the job. If you're applying for a job as a librarian for a professional golf association (yes, such jobs exist), then by all means talk about your interest in golf. If you're applying for any other kind of job, the fact that you're a golfer is probably not relevant.

Your relationship status and children are also not appropriate topics to include in a cover letter. While your personal circumstances and motives are quite honestly none of the hiring committee's business, you may wish to explain your reasons for wanting to relocate. Perhaps your partner is moving for a job, or you need to care for relatives. Search committee members sometimes respond positively to your connection with their location or institution. For example, a prospective employer in Minnesota may wonder if you're really prepared to move there from Arizona. You could include a very brief statement explaining your personal situation, such as "My spouse recently accepted a position in Minnesota." Tread carefully when mentioning any personal information in a cover letter, though. It's always wiser to share too little than too much.

Proofread, proofread, proofread. This seems obvious, but it's amazing how many cover letters show up with typos, misspellings, and other egregious errors. One of the worst: copy/paste mix-ups that result in sentences like "I have always wanted to live in Wisconsin and that is why I am applying for this job at the University of Maine." Don't count on your word processor to call problems to your attention with squiggly red or green lines. Reading your document out loud to yourself will help you catch missing words, awkward language, or leaps in logic. After you've read and reread your cover letter several times, put it aside for a day or two and come back and read it again later with fresh eyes. You're more likely to catch errors after a little time has passed, and you're also better able to imagine how someone who's reading it for the first time will see it. Finally, have someone you trust check it for errors. This is one of the most important professional documents you'll write. A cover letter with errors tells potential employers one of two things: either you aren't able to communicate effectively in writing, or you're careless. Either one could cost you the job.

For a cover letter for an entry-level position, you should aim for a page to a page and a half. A cover letter that's only half a page looks like you didn't put much thought or effort into it. As you advance in your career, your cover letters will probably get longer; if you're applying to be the director of a university library, for example, you'll probably talk about your vision for academic libraries, the role of the library on campus and in higher education as a whole, and other big philosophical issues. For entry-level positions, though, if you find yourself going on and on about your vision, philosophy, and other abstract concepts, you've probably strayed too far afield and need to get back to talking about how your background relates to this job. Hiring managers and search committee members often have to read a large number of letters, so streamline your letter to make it more effective.

CONCLUSION

A cover letter is a critical part of an application packet. It's just as important as your resume, and in many cases it's your introduction to a prospective employer. Devote substantial effort to each cover letter you write, customizing it to the job you're applying for. Rather than just marketing yourself in general terms, explain how your skills and background meet the requirements listed in the vacancy announcement.

The cover letter is just as much about the readers as it is about you. Their primary interest is not why you want the job or how much you'd love to work for them. Focus on the employer's wish list and tell him or her how you can meet those needs.

CHAPTER 10

Interviews

Are you kidding? I'm trained for nothing! I was laughed at in twelve interviews today.

Friends, 1994

For many job seekers, interviewing can be the most intimidating part of the entire process. You're in front of or on the phone with a group of strangers who hold your fate in their hands. They're grilling you, judging you, and making a decision about you that could change your life. It's no wonder most people find interviewing extremely stressful.

Here's something critical to keep in mind: employers don't interview every single person who applies for every single job vacancy they have. If you've been scheduled for a phone or in-person interview, you've passed one or more rounds of screening already. This means that something about your resume or cover letter has piqued their interest enough to make them think you could be a viable candidate for the job. The interview is your opportunity to convince them that their initial hunch was right, and that you're the best person for the position.

You're likely to encounter two different types of interviews: phone interviews and in-person interviews. In general you don't have one instead of the other; usually they take place in sequence. The search committee, library director, HR manager, or whoever is involved in the hiring process reviews all applicants, selects a subset who will get phone interviews, and then some or all of those who are interviewed by phone are invited to interview in person. It's possible that if the pool is small or all the top candidates are local, the library may choose to skip phone interviews and invite all the promising candidates for in-person interviews. It's important to remember that interviews vary widely among different types of libraries; someone interviewing to be a school librarian is likely to have a very different experience from someone interviewing in an academic or special library. Even within a single category of library, interviews will vary from place to place, particularly with special libraries and non-traditional library jobs. We'll describe what a typical interview might be like in different types of libraries and then give some tips and strategies on how to make sure you present yourself well and increase the odds that your interview will be followed by a job offer.

TELEPHONE INTERVIEWS

Telephone interviews serve as a way for a library to find out more about candidates without going through the time and expense of bringing them in for face-to-face interviews. In-person interviews, particularly in academic libraries where they typically last all day and sometimes even longer, require a tremendous amount of time on the part of the hiring organization. During the course of an interview, candidates may meet with dozens of people, all of whose time is valuable. If the library is also paying candidates' travel expenses, in-person interviews become an even bigger investment. To save time and money, libraries typically rely on phone interviews as a pre-screening step to determine which candidates to bring in for in-person interviews. Therefore, you should take a telephone interview just as seriously as a face-to-face interview. Though we'll refer to them as "phone interviews" here, some libraries are now using other technologies like Skype for these distance interviews, and it's likely that use of such technology will increase in the future.

The interviewers will contact you by phone or email to tell you that they'd like to do a phone interview with you and to schedule a time that works for you and for them. They will probably propose some times, and if at all possible, you should agree to one of the times they suggest. If you absolutely can't make any of the times they suggest, it's okay to try to find an alternate time, but it's better if you're flexible and can make your schedule fit theirs, even if it means taking a couple of hours off work, missing a class, or rearranging appointments on your calendar. They will probably have a number of people on the phone at their end, so it's better if you can adjust your schedule instead of making all of them adjust theirs.

How Should You Prepare for a Phone Interview?

You should prepare for a phone interview the same way you would prepare for a face-to-face interview. Reread the vacancy announcement several times to remember the job responsibilities as well as the skills and qualifications the search committee members are looking for. You should also reread the cover letter and resume you sent in because they may ask you for more information or clarification about things you told them in your application packet. Print these documents out and have them on the table in front of you while you're talking to them, or have them up on your screen so you can refer to them during the conversation. Have a glass of water handy in case your throat gets dry, and have a pen and paper nearby so you can jot quick notes to remind yourself of the question, particularly if it's long or has multiple parts, or of things you want to include in your answer. That being said, don't try to write a script ahead of time. You don't know what questions they'll ask you, and you don't want to sound like you're reading off a piece of paper anyway.

It's important to do your homework about the library and, if applicable, the institution it's a part of. You probably did a bit of this before you wrote your resume and cover letter, so take this opportunity to delve deeper and learn more about the organization. For example, if the job is at a university, look at the library's and the university's Web sites, particularly any news, blogs, or "About Us" pages. This will give you an idea of any big projects they are working on, what they're excited about, and what they consider important. You may not get a chance to talk about any of these things during the phone interview, but it will be helpful background information, and it may give you an idea of things they might ask you about. Since they will have scheduled the phone interview in advance rather than calling you out of the blue, make sure you're someplace quiet where you'll be able to talk without distractions or without distracting others. It is best if you can be at home; don't have them call you on your cell phone at a coffee shop, outside, or at a bar on Karaoke Wednesday. It's better to have them call you on a landline if possible, to cut down on the chances of poor reception or a dropped call.

What Should You Expect during a Phone Interview?

A phone interview typically lasts about half an hour, during which time all candidates will probably be asked the same five or six questions. Who's on the other end of the line may depend on what kind of library the job is at. For an academic library, it's likely you'll be speaking to the members of the search committee; at a school or special library, you may only talk to the hiring supervisor, library director, or HR representative. Whoever initiates the call will begin by making sure it's still a good time to talk and then introducing each person so you'll know who you're speaking to. They will probably also tell you about how long they expect the call to last; jot down the projected end time on your paper so you can keep track of how much time has passed and how much time is left.

After the introductions are complete, they'll begin asking you a series of questions. If there's a group of people on the other end of the line, they may go around the table taking turns asking you questions, or they may select one person to ask all of them. It's impossible to predict exactly what they'll ask you, but the questions will likely be centered on how your experience has prepared you for the job and why you think you're a strong candidate. They may ask you to briefly describe your background or why you are interested in the position, so you should be prepared to answer those questions. They may also ask you how you would handle a hypothetical situation you might face in the job, or to describe a time you did X, Y, or Z. For example, if the job involves reference, they may ask you about a time you encountered a difficult patron or a tricky question; if the job involves Web development or programming, they may ask you to describe a Web site you've designed or a script you wrote to perform a particular task. Even if they don't ask you to describe a time when you did whatever, it's a good idea to work that kind of information into your response to one or two of the questions. Don't go over-board with illustrations, though; unless they ask for it, don't turn every response into "Let Me Tell You about the Time I Did This Awesome Thing."

At the end of the call, they may ask you if you have any questions for them. This point will come up several times during this chapter because it will come up several times during your interview process, so we'll tell you now: unless you have decided you absolutely do not want the job under any circumstances, your response to "Do you have any questions for us?" should *never* be "No."

You may want to ask a question about something that came up earlier in the conversation, or about a responsibility that's mentioned in the vacancy announcement that didn't come up during their questions. For example, you might say, "I see in the job posting that the person in this position serves as a member of the library's User Services Committee. Could you tell me a little bit about that group?" Tiffany Eatman Allen (University of North Carolina at Chapel Hill) said, "A candidate who asks relevant, intelligent questions is seen as being well-prepared, intellectually curious, and engaged with the process and the profession." A phone interview is not the time to ask about salary, vacation time, or benefits, however. This is also not the time to ask a question that is very long and involved.

Remember how the interviewers told you about how long the interview would last, and you wrote down the approximate end time on your paper? If you've already asked one question and they ask "Any other questions?" it's okay to ask one more question if there's still time left. For example, if the call was expected to end at 1:30, and after your first question it's only 1:24, it's fine to ask another question if they offer you the opportunity. You shouldn't ask more than two questions, though, and if they don't offer to answer more questions, don't ask any more. Their time is valuable, and they may have a phone call scheduled with the next candidate immediately after yours, so don't keep them over the allotted time and don't keep asking questions if it's apparent that they're trying to wrap up.

At the end of the call, they'll thank you for your time and should give you an idea of what the next step in the process will be. It may be vague, such as, "You'll be hearing from us again soon," or it may be more specific, such as, "We expect to be contacting candidates early next week to schedule on-campus interviews." If they're vague, don't take that as a sign that you did poorly or they didn't like you; it may be that they just don't know yet what the next steps will be. Thank them for their time and close with something positive like "I look forward to hearing from you."

Tips for a Good Phone Interview

Phone interviews can be difficult for everyone, including the people on the other end of the line. Many employers hate doing phone interviews but see them as a necessary evil. The group of people you're speaking to may be crammed around a conference table, craning their necks to hear and talk into a speakerphone. Without visual cues of body language and facial expressions, it can be hard for everyone to know what's going on. Don't worry if you feel awkward, because frequently *everybody* feels that way during phone interviews. There are some things you can do to make things go more smoothly and to make everyone feel more comfortable, though.

If the people at the other end are on a speakerphone, it can be difficult to hear them or for them to hear you. After the introductions at the start of the call, they may ask you "Can you hear us all right?" You may want to respond with something like, "Yes, I can hear you fine, thanks. Can you hear me?" Listen carefully. Remember you are supposed to be in a quiet place; however, if you really can't hear part of a question, politely ask them to repeat it. Speak clearly, but don't yell into the phone unless they keep telling you they can't hear you. Some people find that it helps them project their voices if they stand up during a phone interview; if you do this, don't walk around while you're talking to them. If you choose to sit, sit upright in a straight-back chair; don't talk to them while you're sprawled across the couch or lying in bed staring at the ceiling. Some people even find that it helps them get into the interview mindset if they're dressed in business attire during the phone call. Of course, if you're using some kind of technology where they can see you during the call, a professional appearance at least on the parts of you they can see is essential.

They may ask you long questions with several parts. To help yourself remember and respond to everything, jot notes on your paper as they ask. As you're wrapping up your answer to a long question, it's fine to ask, "Did I answer everything?"

Because you can't see the interviewers' facial expressions or body language, it can be difficult to judge how things are going, or even if you understood the question correctly and are talking about the right thing. Feel free to ask for clarification before you begin your answer, but don't respond to every question with another question. It's better to answer as well as you can and end with something like "Did I answer your question?" or, if you've given an example, "Is that the sort of thing you were asking about?"

Pace yourself. Don't spend too much time answering any one question. They may have told you at the beginning of the call how long it would last and how many questions they were going to ask you. Use that information and a clock to keep things moving. If they tell you they're going to ask you six questions in 30 minutes, don't spend 10 minutes answering the first question. As you're speaking, stop to take a breath between sentences from time to time; it will keep you from getting out of breath, and it will also give them a chance to interrupt if they're ready to move on or they need to correct you because you misunderstood the question.

After they ask a question, it's good to pause a second before you begin answering to take a sip of water and compose your thoughts. Sometimes people get nervous during interviews and immediately start spewing out an answer without knowing where they're going with it. It's better to have a flight plan including a destination in mind before you take off. Listen to what you're saying and avoid repeating yourself or talking in circles, as well as fillers such as "like," "um," and "you know."

Because you can't see them and they can't see you, humor during a phone interview can be tricky. Being ironic or sarcastic may rub them the wrong way, or they may not even be able to tell you're joking based solely on the tone of your voice. Don't be afraid to show your personality, but remember that this is a professional conversation with people you're hoping will give you a job, not a casual chat with your friends.

IN-PERSON INTERVIEWS

After phone screenings are complete, the library will select candidates to invite for in-person interviews. While phone interviews tend to be similar across libraries, in-person interviews vary greatly; those at academic libraries tend to be very different from those at public libraries, or at school libraries, and so on. We'll describe some of the various types of interviews and then give some general tips on how to do your best.

Academic Libraries

On-campus interviews at academic libraries are long. Sometimes, they are *very* long. Typically they begin with dinner with members of the search committee or other staff, followed by a full day of meetings the next day. Why are these interviews so long? College and university libraries can be very large and organizationally complex. Their librarians usually work with many staff across the libraries and, often, with others on campus. Everyone who will be working with the successful candidate wants the chance to meet with him or her during the interview, which results in a long day.

All academic libraries handle their interviews differently, but a candidate for a librarian position might typically have meetings with six to eight different individuals or groups during the day. Meetings could include a combination of these people:

SKYPE INTERVIEWS

by Tiffany Eatman Allen (co-author, Career Q&A with the Library Career People)

Because of the expenses of money and time associated with in-person interviews, many institutions will have an initial round of screening interviews. These have most often been conducted by telephone, but with increasing access to technologies, some institutions are trying videoconferencing or online services, like Skype.

Preparing for a Skype interview is very similar to preparing for a telephone interview or an in-person interview. You'll need to know a lot about the job you're applying for and how your skills and experience match the needs of the position. You'll want to have a glass of water, your application materials (vacancy announcement, cover letter, resume), something to write with and to write on, and a list of a questions to ask the search committee or interview panel when presented with the opportunity. As with a phone interview, make sure you're in a quiet space without interruptions. Turn off home phones, work phones, cell phones, email alerts, and music to prevent distracting background noises.

The most significant difference with Skype as compared to a telephone interview is that you will be seen by your interviewers. Appropriate interview attire is a must, as is a neat, tidy, and organized work space. You don't want a lot of visible clutter: make sure your background is tidy and interview-appropriate, with no piles of laundry or dirty dishes behind you.

One of the hardest things to do, but a really nice touch if you can pull it off, is to look into the "eye" of the camera, not at your screen. Looking at your screen seems natural, because that's where you see the others interviewing you. Unfortunately, that results in no "eye contact"—you appear to be looking down or off to the side. If you can look directly at the camera, at least most of the time, it will appear to the viewer that you're looking right at them. Of course, you can refer down to your notes if you need to, but try to make some direct eye contact during each of the questions. You'll seem self-confident, natural, and at ease with the interviewers, which makes for a better conversation and a stronger interview.

- The position's immediate supervisor
- Members of the department in which the position will be working
- An associate or assistant university librarian or someone else higher up the organizational chart

- The university librarian or dean of libraries
- Library human resources personnel
- The committee that deals with tenure, if librarians at the institution have such status

Depending on the type of position, there will likely be other meetings or sessions during the day. Positions with public service or instructional responsibilities or significant supervisory duties may be expected to give a presentation to all staff which is then followed by a question-and-answer time. If the position serves as a liaison to one or more academic departments or units on campus, there will likely be a meeting with members of those groups. A cataloger who will specialize in particular languages or disciplines may meet with the appropriate subject librarians. If the position includes supervisory responsibilities, there will probably be a meeting with the staff who will be reporting to the individual. You will probably get a brief tour of the library sometime during the day, including a look at the office or cubicle where the successful candidate will be working.

The day usually starts around 8:00 or 8:30, and each of the sessions typically lasts 30–45 minutes, up to an hour. Meetings are usually scheduled back to back with no time in between; the candidate may have several sessions in a row in the same conference room, with different groups or individuals coming in and out for each meeting. The interview schedule also usually includes a 15-minute break sometime in the morning and again in the afternoon. You will have time for lunch, during which a small group of staff usually takes the candidate out to eat somewhere on campus or nearby. The day typically wraps up around 4:00 or 5:00.

"Throughout the day-long interview process, there will be several opportunities to chat casually with your interviewers—at lunch, walking to meetings, during breaks and dinner," said Tiffany Eatman Allen. "Remember you are always being interviewed; nothing is 'off the record,' so stick to safe topics about the library, the geographic region, et cetera. Be warm and personable, but professional and respectful."

This interview schedule may sound grueling, and to be honest, it is. Being "on" all day is exhausting, and by the early afternoon you will start to feel like you are running a marathon. Endurance is a big part of success in academic interviews. Can you still keep your act together and talk somewhat sensibly by 3:00 p.m.? The good news is that time will probably feel like it's going pretty fast, especially if the interview is going well. None of the meetings last too long, and there is so much going on that it may feel like a blur at times, especially when adrenaline kicks in. You'll probably be surprised at how quickly the day goes. Also remember that all the librarians you meet with during the day went through the same process before they were hired, so they will feel sympathetic towards you and will, hopefully, go out of their way to try to make you feel comfortable and make the day go as smoothly as possible. That said, it's up to you to make sure you maintain a consistent level of energy, interest, and enthusiasm throughout the day.

Because you will be meeting with different people and groups throughout the day, you will probably be asked the same question several times in different sessions. It's okay to give the same answer more than once. If it's a question that can reasonably have multiple answers, such as, "Tell us about a time you did X," it's also fine to give different examples each time. Before answering, it's all right to good-naturedly acknowledge that you've discussed this earlier in the day, particularly if one or more of the people who've already heard it are in the room—"Oh, this is something Noah and I had an interesting conversation about at lunch"—but it's easier and safer to just answer the question as if it's the first time you've been asked about it.

Public Libraries

Interviews at public libraries tend to be much shorter than those at academic libraries. Public library interviews may be as short as 45 minutes or as long as half a day, but they typically last 1 or 2 hours. Public libraries frequently use panel interviews, in which the candidate sits in a room with a group of people who ask them questions. The panel interview may be supplemented with separate meetings with other staff members, such as the library's human resources people, the director, or potential colleagues in the department or branch.

"If there is a panel, they take turns asking questions, usually in a clockwise manner," said April Pavis.

> Look at the interviewer when he or she is reading the question, then respond to them using their name. After that first sentence, look at the rest of the panel to continue your response. Be direct and confident. Not everyone on the interview panel will read your cover letter, so if the panelists ask you a question that you know you referenced in your cover letter, answer it as though none of them had read it because it is likely they didn't.

Like their academic counterparts, public library interviews rely heavily on questions of the "Tell us about a time you did X" or "What would you do if Y happened?" varieties. Because they are issues that frequently come up in public libraries, it's likely you'll be asked about censorship, books being challenged, and privacy issues.

Public library interviews can vary greatly depending on the type of job and the responsibilities it involves. It's possible you may be taken to see multiple branches of a public library system. If you're interviewing for a children's or youth services position, you may be asked to lead a mock storytelling session. You should be given an idea of what to expect in advance so you can come prepared.

School Libraries

Interviews for school librarian positions are similar in many ways to public library interviews. They are typically fairly short, lasting half a day or less. You will likely meet with the principal and any other staff who may work in the library or media center; if the school is part of a larger system, you may meet with the district's library services coordinator, other district administrators, or librarians from other schools in the system. You may also meet with teachers or parents at the school.

As with public libraries, you will likely be asked a series of "what if" and "tell us about a time . . ." questions. Again, common questions may involve a parent challenging a book that he or she thinks should be removed from the library, or balancing a child's right to privacy with a parent's right to know what his or her child is doing. School librarians act as teachers, so you may be asked about library instruction ideas, lesson plans, classroom management, and teaching skills. You'll be asked about how you work with children, such as how you might deal with a student who is acting out in the library. You may also be asked to do a mock lesson or story time.

Alma Ramos-McDermott described some potential interview questions.

Some common interview questions ask about types of lessons you've taught, teaching experience, or ways you would improve an existing scenario, like being given the current summer reading list and asking what you would do to improve it. Another question might ask what you would do in a particular situation to discipline a student who was acting out in your class, or how you would promote the library and make it exciting for students. Another question might ask how you would involve teachers in your library.

Special Libraries and Non-library Positions

It's something of a cliché, but special libraries are, well, special. No two special libraries are alike, and their interviewing practices vary as much as the libraries themselves do. Interviewing will be quite different for librarian positions in a law firm, a hospital, a government agency, and a correctional facility. Interviews are also very different in non-library environments such as vendors, publishers, or museums. Because there's no such thing as a typical interview in a special library or non-library environment, we can only give a few examples of what you might experience while interviewing for these types of jobs.

An interview in a special library or non-library may consist of a single short meeting with one person, a couple of sessions that total a half day, or a day-long marathon that's similar to an academic interview. You may be expected to give a presentation or meet with a series of individuals and groups, some of whom may know little or nothing about libraries.

"We do require our candidates to do a presentation," said Susan Scheiberg (RAND Corporation). "We do the interviews by videoconference so library staff in our other location can participate; this provides another challenge for the candidate."

These types of environments often employ solo librarians; that is, the library, if there is one, will be a one-person operation. Therefore, you'll have to be extra careful to keep your audience in mind and avoid library jargon and acronyms. You may be the only librarian in the room; remember that and choose your words carefully. Put yourself in the interviewer's shoes, if you can, so that you translate how your information management expertise can help him or her become more productive.

Special libraries and non-library environments require librarians who are especially flexible and who think creatively, and this unpredictability is reflected in their interviews. Perhaps more than other types of libraries, you have to be prepared to think on your feet and expect the unexpected when interviewing for these types of jobs. For example, candidates for cataloging positions at a book vendor may be asked to take a brief cataloging test during the interview. Interviewees at some organizations or agencies may be subject to strict security measures and may have to be accompanied closely throughout the day. Being able to take unexpected or stressful situations in stride during an interview for these types of jobs will help you demonstrate that you'll be able to face surprises on the job without buckling under the pressure.

"Many of our questions are situational so that we can ascertain if a person has the analytical skills to do the job," said Dawn Krause. "Be prepared to come up with scenarios where you've worked on a team or a scenario where you've had a difficult time but came out of it with a great lesson learned. This gives employers an idea if you have good judgment as well."

GENERAL INTERVIEW TIPS

No matter what type of position or environment you're interviewing for, there are a number of things you can do to make things go smoothly and improve your odds of getting the job.

Do Your Homework

We touched on this back in the section about phone interviews, but it's even more important when you're preparing for an in-person interview. Don't show up unprepared. Finding information is what librarians do; you need to learn as much as you can about the library or organization before you show up for the interview.

Spend time looking at their Web site in more depth than you did when you prepared for your phone interview. Learn about the history, mission, and structure of the institution. Find out what new projects or initiatives are underway. This kind of preparation will help you know what people are talking about during the day and also allow you to ask more relevant, intelligent questions.

Learn more about the librarians and staff at the organization. Read articles that the librarians have published to get a better sense of their research interests and personalities. Knowing more about the people you're talking with can also help calm your nerves during the interview, because you can relate better to them as real people rather than Intimidating Interviewers.

Come Prepared

You can bring a few things with you to make yourself feel more prepared. You should bring a copy of the resume and cover letter you sent when you applied for the job. It's likely someone will ask you a question about something they've seen in your application packet, so it will be useful if you also have a copy of what they're looking at in front of you. You should also bring anything the employer may have sent you in advance, such as a copy of your schedule, the library's mission statement, or an organizational chart.

In addition to the printed material you bring with you, it's possible that you will also be given documents during the day. To avoid having to carry a stack of loose paper around all day, you may want to invest in an inexpensive but nice-looking portfolio. This will also give you a place to keep a legal pad and pens so you can take notes during the day. You shouldn't take lengthy or thorough notes at any time during the day. Remember, you're the candidate, not the minute-taker; but it may be useful to jot down brief notes to yourself here and there throughout the day, even if it's just the names of the people you meet in each session.

Of course, it's always a good idea to bring essentials such as mints (not gum), tissues, or aspirin. Keep these things to a minimum, however. You don't want to look like you've packed for a hike on the Appalachian Trail.

Dress to Impress

People often wonder what appropriate dress for an interview is. It's true that libraries are often more casual work environments than many others, but you should always dress up for an interview. If you hate dressing up, take heart in the fact that your interview may be the last time your future coworkers ever see you in a suit. If in doubt, overdress. It's better to err on the side of being too conservative than being too casual or wacky. Make sure your clothes are ironed and your shoes are shiny, or at least clean. This may seem obvious, but you'd be surprised how many candidates show up for interviews looking like they slept in their clothes or stopped to do some gardening on the way in. "Making a great first impression is critical," said Blane Dessy. "Make sure that you have some nice interview clothes. Being overdressed is better than being underdressed."

Don't feel awkward if you arrive for your interview and find you're dressed much more formally than everyone else. That's normal: you're the candidate. Seeing what staff members are wearing may give you an idea of what typical attire for the workplace is, although it's possible they've all dressed up to impress you, too.

It's okay to express yourself through your clothes and accessories, but you don't want what you're wearing to be distracting. If, at the end of the day, your outfit is the main thing people remember about you, something has gone wrong.

Keep Up Your Energy

Maintaining a constant, appropriate level of energy throughout your interview can be challenging, particularly if it lasts all day. Pace yourself; don't burn out by expending all your energy in the morning. Your afternoon sessions are just as important as the morning ones. You want to keep up your level of enthusiasm without being manic or frenzied. The people who are interviewing you will have to spend a lot of time with you if they hire you, possibly over a period of years, so you don't want to scare them off by coming across as frantic or just plain "too much." At the same time, you don't want to slouch through the day like a zombie.

Your interviewers may have built break periods into your day to give you a chance to sit down and have a cup of coffee or drink of water; if not, take advantage of breaks between sessions to go to the restroom to collect your thoughts and check yourself in the mirror. Remember, though, that even during meals and break periods, you are still "on." Don't get too casual, and remember that nothing you say during the interview day is truly off the record.

Practice Your Presentation

You may be asked to do a presentation or "job talk" as part of your interview. You should receive a question or discussion topic in advance—for example, "Discuss challenges and opportunities in providing electronic access to special collections materials," "Share your vision for the future of library instruction," or "Discuss the challenge of providing library services to at-risk students."

You will also be told how long your presentation should last. Make sure you don't go over this time limit. This session will probably have time built in at the end for questions from the audience; for example, it might be a 30-minute presentation followed by 15 minutes for questions from your audience. One of the worst things you can do is to run over on the presentation and not leave time for questions from the audience. This may make the audience feel you're trying to hide something by not letting them ask questions and may also give the impression that you can't follow directions.

Practice your talk repeatedly, timing yourself and cutting as necessary. Don't try to cram too much into the presentation; you don't want the audience to feel overwhelmed by a flood of information. Periodically stop to take breaths and a sip of water to slow yourself down and give the audience a chance to think about what you're saying.

Much of the advice that applies to telephone interviews also applies to the question-and-answer period of a presentation. Take a second to think about what you're going to say before you begin your answer. Don't spend too much time answering any one question, and ask something like "Does that answer your question?" when you finish a response to ensure that you were on the right track. Make sure you thank the audience for coming at the beginning of the session, and for their attention at the end.

Be Nice ... and Positive

This may seem obvious, but it's absolutely critical: be pleasant. The people who are meeting with you during your interview aren't just trying to decide whether you can do the job; they're also deciding whether you're someone they want to work with, possibly for a long, long time. "I've become convinced that the biggest part of landing a job, if your experience is mostly in line with the requirements, is having a personality that most people in the new place like," said Beatrice Caraway (Trinity University).

Be polite, friendly, and outgoing, while maintaining professional decorum. Your potential coworkers want to get to know you, and they want someone who's fun or at least pleasant to work with, so let your personality shine, but remember you're at a job interview, not a cocktail party. Make eye contact, shake hands, and thank people for coming. Listen to what people are saying; don't spend all your time thinking about what you're going to say next.

Whatever you do, don't say negative things about your current or former jobs. Remember, the library world is a small one; the people you're meeting with may know the people you're trashing. Finally, if people think you're just plain negative, they won't want to work with you. There are probably already some complainers in the organization, and they don't want more.

" 'Be polite and respectful to everyone' is such obvious interview advice," Ginger Williams said.

> I'm always amazed to see good candidates kill their chances by being condescending toward non-librarian staff. We remember a candidate who was such a clear front runner that we didn't plan to invite anyone else to campus for an interview. He carefully repeated names and positions during each meeting, then gave curt answers to questions from non-librarians, ignored their follow-up questions, didn't make eye contact with them, and started his own questions with phrases like "from a librarian's perspective." We called our second candidate to arrange a campus interview before the first candidate's plane was off the ground.

You should also express enthusiasm for the job. Filling this vacancy is important to your potential employers and coworkers, so they want to feel like it's important to you, too. "A good attitude gets you far. Paired with a thoughtful demeanor it will get you even further," said Samantha Schmehl Hines. "If you don't necessarily have the experience but are able to speak cogently on topics and present ideas, you may get further than someone who has already done the job but can't explain why it's important or seem all that excited about it."

Interviews can be draining, and sometimes unexpected events—a flight delay, a dash through the rain in your brand-new interview suit—can unsettle you. Put a positive spin on negative situations. "Use a negative experience to show your problem-solving skills," said Diane Calvin. "Many of my colleagues still remember a new library school graduate who had a bad hotel experience on the morning of the interview. The candidate turned it into a humorous anecdote that showed her determination to make it to the interview. It showed us she could take setbacks in stride and not let personal inconveniences interfere with a business situation. And we hired her."

Ask Questions

At some point during the day, and probably more than once, you will be asked, "Do you have any questions for us?" This question typically comes at the end of a session, and you will often hear it more towards the end of the day. Remember, the answer to "Do you have questions for us?" should never, ever be "No." Asking questions shows that you have been paying attention and truly thinking about what you are seeing and hearing.

"Never, and I mean never, come into an interview with me and not have questions about the job or the place of employment," Dawn Krause said. "When employers ask you, 'Do you have any questions for us?,' they're trying to gauge your interest level. No questions translates that you're not very interested or that you aren't assessing how the job might fit you. Interviews are a two-way street. As a new grad, you might feel like you don't have the power to be choosy and ask questions, but you absolutely do!"

For example, if people have mentioned a major project or initiative the library is working on, a good question might be, "How do you see the person in this position being involved in that project?" If no one has mentioned such projects, you could ask, "What is the library working on or considering doing that you are excited about?"

A good all-purpose question, particularly when you're meeting with a group of people such as the department you would be working in should you get the job, is, "What do you like about working here?" The responses to this question can be very telling: it's a good sign if they are able to easily come up with things they enjoy about their jobs, the environment, and each other. On the other hand, if no one can think of anything they like about working there, then you should ask yourself whether it's an emotionally healthy environment and whether you'd like to be part of it.

Job seekers often wonder when they should ask questions they have about salary, benefits, retirement, vacation time, and other nitty-gritty aspects of the job. At some point during the day, you may meet with the library's human resources manager, who will probably go over much of this information with you. If you don't meet with an HR representative, you can ask these questions of the hiring supervisor, director, principal, or someone else in a position of authority. Use common sense; for example, don't ask questions about salary or ask for details about benefits with the members of the department in which you'll be working. They may not know the answers, and more important, talking about money can be awkward or off-putting if done at the wrong time or with the wrong audience.

Remember: You're Interviewing Them, Too

Many interviewees, particularly new graduates, feel that the purpose of an interview is to say and do whatever it takes to get a job offer. While you obviously do want to have a successful interview, it's important to remember that you're interviewing them, too.

What this means is that while they are trying to decide whether you'd be a good fit for their organization, you're trying to decide whether their organization would be a good fit for you. During the course of the interview, whether it's an hour long or a day and a half, keep your eyes and ears open and pay attention to what the mood and environment feel like. How do the people you meet seem to feel about their jobs, and how do they get along and interact with each other? Do they seem to like each other? Do they enjoy their work? Are they enthusiastic about what they're doing? Are they welcoming? "We know that candidates are interviewing us as well, so we want the interview to go as smoothly as possible, and for each candidate to have a great experience with us," said Tiffany Eatman Allen.

Also, your interview is an opportunity for you to find out more about the job, including what all the duties are and what a typical day would be like. Ask yourself if this is really a job you can see yourself enjoying. At the end of the day or even earlier you should have a good idea of whether you still really want the job or not. Be yourself, and trust your instincts.

AFTER THE INTERVIEW

It is extremely unlikely you will get a job offer before you leave. Time will pass. The organization may be interviewing other candidates after you, or perhaps you are the last in a series of candidates. After completing the interviews, the search committee, HR director, or whoever is running the search will probably solicit comments from the people who met with you, attended your presentation, or had any other kind of interaction with you. Then they will meet, possibly more than once, and probably write and submit some kind of report to the director, board, or whoever's in charge. The report will summarize the strengths and weaknesses of the candidates and may or may not make a recommendation. All this takes time, particularly in academic libraries, so if you don't hear anything back immediately, don't interpret that to mean you did poorly or they didn't like you.

It's a good idea to send a thank-you note after your in-person interview. It's a professional courtesy that demonstrates you're thoughtful and conscientious. It also shows that you're still interested in the position. Finally, it will set you apart from those candidates who don't take the time and effort to send a note.

You only need to send a single thank-you note; don't send one to everyone you met with. If you met with a lot of people during the day, address your note to the person with whom you spent the most time. This may be the chair of the search committee, the HR manager, the library director, the hiring supervisor, or someone else. Make sure you acknowledge that you met others during the day, with something like "Please thank everyone who took the time to meet with me."

Your note doesn't need to be anything elaborate. It should be short; three or four sentences is fine, and you shouldn't treat it as if it's another cover letter. Thank them for their time, tell them you enjoyed meeting with them and learning about the organization, and express that you're still very interested in the position. You may take the opportunity to follow up on a point that was raised during the interview. As with the cover letter, end with a positive statement: "I look forward to hearing from you; please don't hesitate to contact me if I can answer any questions or give you further information about my interest in the position."

It's all right to send a thank-you note by email, but it's nicer to send an actual letter through the mail. A handwritten note is nice if you have decent handwriting, but if your handwriting is illegible, then type the note. The important thing is that you've taken the time to thank them. Send the note as soon as possible after the interview, while you're still fresh in their minds and, hopefully, before they have made a decision.

CONCLUSION

Interviews are stressful, whether they take place by phone, via videoconference, or in person. While it's likely your interview will follow one of a few basic patterns, you should be prepared to adapt to any surprise you encounter. Before the interview, do your homework so that you feel prepared and confident. On the day of the interview, be positive, energetic, friendly, and professional, keeping in mind that you're evaluating the people you meet just as much as they're interviewing you. By taking some control over the process, you increase the odds that you will be receiving a job offer soon.

CHAPTER 11

Your New Job

You hired me. I can't help it if your standards are lax.
Pirates of the Caribbean: Dead Man's Chest, 2006

Congratulations! You have a job offer! Now what?

EVALUATING AN OFFER

Evaluate how you feel about the organization, the people you interviewed with, the location, the salary, the job duties, and so on. "Your job search involves not only finding the right position, but also the right kind of library that will support your professional goals and allow you to flourish," wrote Nancy Cunningham in her article "In Search of an Emotionally Healthy Library."

Did you feel comfortable with the people you met during the interview? Did the work sound interesting? Consider whether you can afford to live on the salary. Is the salary comparable to similar jobs in the area? Would you like living there? Use your network to find out more about the organization and the location.

NEGOTIATING

Should you negotiate? If so, what do you negotiate for? How do you negotiate?

When you are presented with a job offer, ask for 24 hours to think it over, even if you're sure you want the job. Compare the compensation and benefits to your salary needs. Although many librarian salaries are not negotiable, sometimes they are. If the salary is set, you may instead have the ability to negotiate for other benefits such as flex time, professional association dues, travel funding, upgraded computer equipment, parking spaces, or relocation expenses.

Employers respond more favorably to requests that are based on professional rather than personal needs. Keep your requests and expectations reasonable, especially if this is your first professional position. Decide what you are willing to accept. If the employer does not give you what you want, be prepared to accept his or her terms, or to decline the job offer. In either case, be gracious.

You may also need to negotiate a start date. Your new employer may suggest a date or may ask you when you will be able to begin. It's likely that your new employer and coworkers will want you to start as soon as possible, especially if the position has been vacant for a while. Also, they have no doubt realized you are an awesome person and can't wait to be around you every day. Don't feel pressured to accept the first start date they propose if it seems too rushed for you, particularly if you will have to find a new place to live, then pack and move. At the same time, make a concerted effort to work with your new employer to begin as soon as you comfortably can.

DECLINING (OR DELAYING) AN OFFER

Accepting is easy; but what if you decide you don't want the job? Call the person who offered you the job and decline graciously. Be professional and polite. Don't badmouth the organization to others. Don't share information about the interview that might be considered confidential. Word spreads quickly in the library field.

It's possible you may get a job offer while you're waiting to hear from other institutions. It's okay to be honest: say you're looking at several options and request a little extra time, but be prepared to make a decision. If Library A offers you a job while you're still waiting to hear back from Library B after interviewing there, call your contact (the HR manager, hiring supervisor, etc.) at Library B and tell him or her you've received another offer. Ask where the process stands and how soon you might be hearing from them. If they're interested in you, they may be able to expedite the process to keep from losing you.

Throughout the process, make sure you're gracious and cordial. You don't want potential employers to feel like you're trying to play them against each other, manipulate them, or threaten them. At some point, you may have to make a difficult decision and take a risk or not. If Library A wants a decision and Library B isn't ready to make one, or won't tell you where things stand, you'll have to decide whether you want the sure thing or whether you'll decline it for a "maybe."

RESIGNING YOUR CURRENT JOB

Tell your supervisor you're leaving in a gracious, professional manner. Be prepared for your supervisor or coworkers to feel disappointed or possibly a little betrayed; after all, you're leaving them. At least initially, they may feel a sense of "You like them better than you like us." Of course, if you're a student, your employer is no doubt expecting you to look for a professional position and will probably be thrilled at your news.

It's customary to give your employer several weeks' notice before you leave your current job. A good rule of thumb is to give them at least one pay period's notice. If you're paid biweekly, you should give at least two weeks' notice. Particularly if you've had a very positive work experience, it's also nice to write your boss a thank-you letter or note. While you're at it, tell everyone who served as a reference during your search about your new job, and thank them profusely for their help.

It's easy to slack off when you're leaving a job. It's the grown-up version of the "senioritis" high school students suffer in their final semester before graduation. Keep working hard during your last few weeks. If you can reasonably finish any projects you've been working on, put in the extra effort to wrap them up, and do a good job on them. When you go, you want to leave behind a positive impression, not a big mess that somebody else will have to clean up.

If you are not happy in your current job, guard against expressing bitterness or criticism. Don't burn any bridges. As much as you may fantasize about telling everybody off on your way out the door, don't do it. Posting a day-by-day countdown on a social networking site ("Three more days and I'm outta this dump!") is not a great idea. Maintain positive connections with your supervisor and coworkers. Remember how small the library world is; you'll probably see these people again.

STARTING A NEW JOB

As you start your new job, remember what employers said they were looking for: enthusiasm, initiative, flexibility, collaboration, communication, innovation, vision, a positive attitude, and a service orientation. During your first year on the job, learn about the environment, the people, and the culture. Listen more than you talk. If you don't understand something, ask. Volunteer for opportunities to serve on committees outside your immediate area of responsibility. This allows you to broaden your network, expand your skill set, and gain diverse experience that can prepare you for the next stage in your career.

However, don't get so caught up in expanding your repertoire that you lose track of your real job, that is, what you were hired to do. Establish a reputation as a conscientious, responsible team member: show up when you're expected, fulfill your job responsibilities, meet deadlines, and follow through on commitments.

As many employers pointed out, one of your greatest strengths as a recent graduate is your enthusiasm. Even though you have lots of great ideas, though, don't charge into your new workplace like a bull in a china shop. If you're in a position where you have the authority to make major changes, learn the lay of the land and work to build consensus before you start changing things. Even if the place is a mess, your coworkers may not respond well to a newcomer immediately turning everything upside down. No matter what your job role, be tactful when suggesting changes. Listen and learn how things have been done; learn how change is typically implemented (for example, how many levels of approval do you have to go through?); propose changes in positive, diplomatic terms. Be gracious; don't whine if your ideas are not accepted. Don't become known as a complainer, because your future proposals will be taken less seriously.

Any organization, no matter how healthy, will have some complicated politics and interpersonal relationships. Tread lightly as you begin your job. Keep your eyes and ears open. You will likely find out that some of your coworkers don't like each other, and they may try to make you take sides. Be cordial, but don't let yourself get drawn into the quagmire. Don't spread gossip; while it can be useful to keep an ear on the rumor mill, be very careful not to contribute to it.

On a much more positive note, you will also quickly find out who the stars of the organization are: who gets things done, who is well respected, and whom everybody loves. Find ways to meet these people, work with them, and observe the behaviors that have gained the respect of others. Also make an effort to get to know your coworkers on a more personal level by occasionally eating lunch with them in the staff lounge or going out to coffee with them. Even though you may not become best friends with everyone, your coworkers will play a large role in your daily work life and your career. Building cordial relationships with them will make work more productive, more pleasant, and more fun.

"School really doesn't teach us how to adjust to life as part of an institution," said Ava Iuliano.

> There are political and interpersonal nuances that few of us are prepared for, particularly when we join a large institution. I've had to learn how people communicate and adjust my own reactions based on considerations for context. This is something I was not prepared to do, particularly as a new grad. I was largely an island as a grad student. As an employee, I've had to understand myself as part of a larger organism.

CONCLUSION

Everything you've done to this point—your education, work experience, network-building, and job hunt—has led you to your new position. Be proud of yourself! Of course, this is just the beginning. As your career progresses, you'll continue to rely on and further the skills you gained in school and during your job search.

Your network will never be complete; you will continue expanding it for the rest of your life. At your new job, you'll meet new colleagues, patrons, vendors, and other members of your community. As you pursue your involvement in professional associations, you'll keep meeting new and fascinating people. You never know where these new connections will lead you. Keep an open mind; looking for opportunities to move your career in new directions will keep it fresh and interesting.

At the same time, remember that networks are a two-way street, or, perhaps more accurately, a complicated web that spreads out in every direction. Make an effort to help others as much as they help you. Librarianship is extremely collaborative, and the best ideas almost always come from groups. As you grow from a novice to an expert, remember how mentors helped you when you were starting out, and find ways to repay that debt to other new professionals. You don't have to wait until you have many years of experience under your belt. Even at this early stage of your career, you can help students and newer professionals by sharing your experiences in person, on social networks or online forums, or in articles or presentations.

Everything you do in your career builds your professional identity (or, if you'd prefer, your brand). If you manage your professional life thoughtfully, you may be surprised how quickly you establish a reputation that's recognized and respected by your peers. Librarianship is a wonderful, satisfying, important profession. Take control of your career from the very beginning to become an integral member of the community and share your love of information with those around you.

WORK CITED

Cunningham, Nancy. "In Search of an Emotionally Healthy Library," http://www
.liscareer.com (cited October 4, 2011).

Resources

BOOKS

Bridges, Karl. *Expectations of Librarians in the 21st Century*. Westport, CT: Greenwood Publishing, 2003.

Carvell, Linda. *Career Opportunities in Library and Information Science*. New York: Ferguson, 2005.

De Stricker, Ulla, and Jill Hurst-Wahl. *The Information and Knowledge Professional's Career Handbook*. Oxford, UK: Chandos Publishing, 2011.

Dority, G. Kim. *Rethinking Information Work: A Career Guide for Librarians and Other Information Professionals*. Westport, CT: Libraries Unlimited, 2006.

Doucett, Elisabeth. *What They Don't Teach You in Library School*. Chicago: American Library Association, 2010.

Eberts, Marjorie, and Margaret Gisler. *Careers for Bookworms & Other Literary Types*. New York: McGraw-Hill, 2009.

Fourie, Denise K., and David R. Dowell. *Libraries in the Information Age: An Introduction and Career Exploration*. Westport, CT: Libraries Unlimited, 2002.

Gordon, Rachel Singer. *What's the Alternative?: Career Options for Librarians and Info Pros*. Medford, NJ: Information Today, 2008.

Haycock, Ken. *The Portable MLIS*. Westport, CT: Libraries Unlimited, 2008.

Johnson, Sarah L., and Rachel Singer Gordon. *The Information Professional's Guide to Career Development Online*. Medford, NJ: Information Today, 2002.

Kane, Laura Townsend. *Straight from the Stacks: A First-Hand Guide to Careers in Library and Information Science*. Chicago: American Library Association, 2003.

Kane, Laura Townsend. *Working in the Virtual Stacks: The New Library and Information Science*. Chicago: American Library Association, 2011.

Langley, Anne, Edward Gray, and K. T. L. Vaughan. *The Role of the Academic Librarian*. Oxford, UK: Chandos Publishing, 2003.

Lawson, Judy, Joanna Kroll, and Kelly Kowatch. *The New Information Professional: Your Guide to Careers in the Digital Age*. New York: Neal-Schuman, 2010.

McCook, Kathleen De La Pena, Margaret Myers, Blythe Camenson. *Opportunities in Library & Information Science Careers*. New York: McGraw-Hill, 2001.

Neely, Teresa Y. *How to Stay Afloat in the Academic Library Job Pool*. Chicago: American Library Association, 2011.

Nesbeitt, Sarah L., and Rachel Singer Gordon. *The Information Professional's Guide to Career Development Online*. Medford, NJ: Information Today, 2002.

Newlen, Robert. *Resume Writing and Interviewing Techniques That Work!: A How-to-Do-It Manual for Librarians*. New York: Neal-Schuman, 2006.

Pantry, Sheila, and Peter Griffiths. *Your Essential Guide to Career Success*. London, UK: Facet Publishing, 2003.

Perez, Megan Zoe, and Cindy A. Gruwell, editors. *The New Graduate Experience: Post-MLS Residency Programs and Early Career Librarianship*. Westport, CT: Libraries Unlimited, 2010.

Pressley, Lauren. *So You Want to Be a Librarian!* Duluth, MN: Library Juice Press, 2009.

Raddin, Rosemary. *Your Career, Your Life: Career Management for the Information Professional*. Burlington, VT: Ashgate Publishing, 2004.

Sellen, Betty-Carol. *What Else You Can Do with a Library Degree: Career Options for the 90s and Beyond*. New York: Neal-Schuman, 1997.

Shontz, Priscilla K. *Jump Start Your Career in Library and Information Science*. Lanham, MD: Scarecrow Press, 2002.

Shontz, Priscilla K., editor. *The Librarian's Career Guidebook*. Lanham, MD: Scarecrow Press, 2004.

Shontz, Priscilla K., and Richard A. Murray, editors. *A Day in the Life: Career Options in Library and Information Science*. Westport, CT: Libraries Unlimited, 2007.

Taylor, T. Allan, and James Robert Parish. *Career Opportunities in Library and Information Science*. New York: Ferguson, 2009.

Tucker, Cory, and Reeta Sinha. *New Librarian, New Job: Practical Advice for Managing the Transition*. Lanham, MD: Scarecrow Press, 2007.

Watson-Boone, Rebecca. *A Good Match: Library Career Opportunities for Graduates of Liberal Arts Colleges*. Chicago: American Library Association, 2007.

Woodward, Jeannette. *A Librarian's Guide to an Uncertain Job Market*. Chicago: American Library Association, 2011.

ONLINE

ALA JobList: Career Resources. http://joblist.ala.org/modules/jobseeker/jobseekerhomepage.cfm (cited February 22, 2012).

Career Q&A with the Library Career People. http://www.lisjobs.com/careerqa_blog/ (cited February 22, 2012).

INALJ (I Need a Library Job). http://www.inalj.com (cited February 22, 2012).

Infonista. http://infonista.com/ (cited February 22, 2012).

Libgig. http://www.libgig.com/ (cited February 22, 2012).

Library Career Anxiety. http://librarycareeranxiety.tumblr.com/ (cited February 22, 2012).

Librarycareers.org. http://www.ala.org/ala/educationcareers/careers/librarycareerssite/home.cfm (cited February 22, 2012).

LIScareer.com. http://www.liscareer.com/ (cited February 22, 2012).

San José State University School of Library and Information Science. "Job Listing Sites and Resources," http://slisweb.sjsu.edu/resources/career_development/jobsearch_resources.htm (cited February 22, 2012).

Simmons Graduate School of Library and Information Science. "Career Links," http://www.simmons.edu/gslis/careers/resources/links.php (cited February 22, 2012).

INDEX

About the Authors

PRISCILLA K. SHONTZ is editor of the career site LIScareer.com, coeditor of *A Day in the Life: Career Options in Library and Information Science*, editor of *The Librarian's Career Guidebook*, and author of *Jump Start Your Career in Library and Information Science*. She has more than 18 years of experience in academic, public, special, and school libraries. She is a past president of the American Library Association New Members Round Table. Priscilla earned a BS in journalism from the University of Texas at Arlington and an MS in library science from the University of North Texas.

RICHARD A. MURRAY is the metadata librarian in the digital collections program at the Duke University Libraries in Durham, North Carolina. He has more than 15 years of experience as a metadata librarian and as a cataloger specializing in Spanish- and Portuguese-language materials at Duke University, Vanderbilt University, and the University of North Carolina at Chapel Hill. Rich earned a BA in international studies and an MS in library science from the University of North Carolina at Chapel Hill. He is the assistant editor of LIScareer.com and coeditor of *A Day in the Life: Career Options in Library and Information Science*.